Libel Law

A JOURNALIST'S HANDBOOK

Damian McHugh

BARRISTER-AT-LAW

With a foreword by
Mr Justice Peter Kelly, Judge of the High Court

FOUR COURTS PRESS

Set in 11 on 13 point Times for
FOUR COURTS PRESS LTD
Fumbally Lane, Dublin 8, Ireland
e-mail: info@four-courts-press-ie
http://www.four-courts-press.ie
and in North America for
FOUR COURTS PRESS
c/o ISBS, 5824 N.E. Hassalo Street, Portland, OR 97213.

A catalogue record for this title
is available from the British Library.

ISBN 1–85182–640-8

ACKNOWLEDGMENTS
The text of the Defamation Act, 1961 is
reproduced with the permission of the
Controller, Stationery Office, Dublin.

Printed in Ireland
by Betaprint, Dublin.

Foreword

*'The present state of many of our papers is such that it may
be doubted not only whether the compilers know their duty,
but whether they have endeavoured or wished to know it.'*

Dr Samuel Johnson, 'On the Duty of a Journalist'.

It is part of the lot of working journalists that they must carry on their business
in the knowledge that their endeavours may run the risk of offending the
defamation laws. No doubt some find this irksome; others may regard it as
obstructive of their work. But when one considers the enormous power to
damage a reputation contained in the journalist's pen, it can scarcely be denied
that such power must be exercised in circumstances where an effective remedy
is available to those who may be unjustly wronged.

There are many and varied views as to whether the existing law of
defamation requires amendment or not. This is not the place to discuss the
merits of that issue. Whether one likes it or not the law is there and journalists
have to behave in accordance with it or run the risks attendant upon non
compliance.

It is the foolish journalist who does not – to quote Dr Johnson –
'endeavour or wish' to know the law of defamation as part and parcel of
everyday work. It is of course unrealistic to think that every reporter should
have, or even needs to have, the detailed knowledge of a professional lawyer
who practises in the field. Nonetheless the journalist can reasonably be
expected to know enough about the law so as to realise when professional
assistance should be invoked.

It is difficult to find a textbook which can provide such a knowledge to
journalists. The standard textbooks used by lawyers are too specialised to be
of much benefit. What is required is a vade-mecum which provides an

overview of the law tailor-made for the use of journalists. The present work supplies that need admirably.

Damian McHugh has been a journalist for many years. He has an appreciation of the pressures under which they operate. He is also a practising barrister who has taken a particular interest in this topic. He is therefore the ideal person to sketch out the legal landscape against which journalists must work. In this book he has done so in an attractive and digestible fashion. He is a journalist writing for other journalists in a way which imparts legal information in a way uniquely suited to their needs.

In my view he has wholly succeeded in the task which he set himself. In less than one hundred pages of text he has provided not merely an overview of the law of defamation but has incorporated many useful pieces of advice and suggestions, gleaned from his experience as a journalist. He has dealt with court reporting, contempt of court, the law of privacy and other relevant areas.

In my view any journalist who wishes to know his duty as advised by Dr Johnson could not do better than read this very worthwhile book.

Peter Kelly
The High Court

To my wife, Claire,
and to our children,
Damian, Trudi, Avril,
Debbie, Robert and Shane

Contents

Preface

More than a decade has passed since the first edition of this handbook was published. Originally, it was intended as a stop-gap measure to give journalists a working knowledge of defamation law, the offence of contempt of court and court reporting pending what was thought to be the imminent reform of the Defamation Act, 1961. Two years after its publication, the Law Reform Commision under its then President, Mr Justice Ronan Keane, the current Chief Justice, published comprehensive consultation papers on the Civil Law of Defamation and Contempt of Court together with proposals for reform of the law then existing after being requested to carry out this work by a former Attorney General.

Libel Law was the first indigenous handbook on these topics and it quickly went out of print. It ought to have slipped quietly into the background waiting, perhaps, a revision after the much-awaited reform proposals were enacted into law. Years passed, governments changed, newspaper publishers, broadcasters and commentators called for reform. In 1995, the Government's Commission on the Newspaper Industry received submissions on the need for reform. Despite all of this, the basic law of defamation as stated in the 1961 Act remains untouched by the legislator's hand. In the meantime, the culture of libel litigation has grown enormously since this handbook first appeared in 1989. So also has the size of awards. Media law, which incorporates the law of defamation, has become an essential subject on journalism, communication and public relations courses at undergraduate and postgraduate levels throughout the country. Textbooks and other works on media law have been published and have become valuable aids for students in the intervening years.

The appeal of *Libel Law* was not just the fact that it was a first in its field but because it tried to explain in simple, everyday language a complex area of law, written from the perspective of a working journalist, who had latterly qualified as a barrister and was in general practice. Given the absence of legislative reform, an apparent need for a second edition of this handbook presented itself, not just for broadcasting and print journalists but for media, communication and public relations students and their lecturers who want a concise handbook for ease of reference rather than having to wade through a weighty tome.

It was against this background that the idea of a second edition began to germinate. What I have sought to do in this second edition is to revise and up-date developments in the law of defamation and the other areas considered as much as possible. In that context, references from the latest Supreme Court judgments in *De Rossa v. Independent Newspapers plc* (30 July 1999) and *O'Brien v. Mirror Group Newspapers Ltd and Others* (25 October 2000) on the question of libel damages are included in the text. As in the first edition, I have tried to reduce the number of case references throughout in order to keep the text as short and as simple as possible. It would have been very easy to over-write many of the topics but that would have only resulted in defeating the very purpose for which this handbook first came into existence – to make available an easy-to-understand manual designed to be of everyday use to journalists and students.

While expanding on many of the items dealt with in the first edition, I have included a number of new areas in this edition, including cyber-libel and restrictions on court reporting.

I am eternally grateful to my first master, Mr Justice Peter Kelly, who, despite a heavy workload, unhesitatingly agreed to write the Foreword. His imprimatur to this handbook adds considerable value to my modest effort. I am also indebted to Michael Adams of Four Courts Press who was associated with the publication of the first edition. It would be amiss of me not to acknowledge the encouragement I received from colleagues in the Law Library, most especially Mel Christle SC, and the academic staff at the Dublin Institute of Technology, Aungier Street, Dublin, especially David Quinn, Nora French, Michael Foley and, not least, Muiris Mac Conghail, who tactfully pressurised me into writing this second edition before I finally ran out of excuses as to why I should not.

I have addressed the topics covered in this handbook at meetings and workshops with many print and broadcasting journalists in the recent past. They voiced concerns they had in trying to keep within the parameters of the law. If this handbook gives a better understanding of the law it attempts to cover and helps journalists in the process, it will have acheived its objective.

Finally, but most important, I want to acknowledge the support and encouragement given to me by my wife, Claire, and our children during the difficult years following the closure of the Irish Press in 1995. This second edition is a token of my appreciation and is dedicated to them.

Damian McHugh

1

Libel

Arguably our reputation or our good name is the most valuable asset that we as citizens possess. It is acknowledged in *Bunreacht na hÉireann*, which charges the State with the obligation of enacting laws to defend and vindicate the personal rights of the citizen. That provision, in Article 40, section 3, sub-section 1 goes further in sub-section 2 by compelling the State, by its laws, to protect from unjust attack and, in the case of injustice done, vindicate the life, person, *good name*, and property rights of every citizen. Even though the same Article 40, at section 6, guarantees free speech and freedom of the Press, these latter constitutional rights would take second place in any conflict situation with the former such as in our courts.

It is in this context that we look at the law of defamation which attempts to strike a balance between these competing rights. Defamation is a tort, a civil wrong. Other torts include negligence, nuisance, trespass, false imprisonment and nervous shock, all of which involve injuries to either property or to the person. Defamation can be either libel or slander.

Libel is the legal name for defamatory words written, printed, or otherwise permanently represented (such as in a painting or effigy). *Slander* is the term applied to defamatory words uttered by word of mouth, i.e. the spoken word. Broadcasters might question why they are subject to the tort of libel rather than to that of slander. The answer is contained in section 15 of the Defamation Act, 1961, which states: 'For the purposes of the law of libel and slander the broadcasting of words by means of wireless telegraphy shall be treated as publication in permanent form.' Professionally, journalists, therefore, are concerned with libel.

The tort of *defamation* protects interests in reputation. It is the publication to a third person of matter 'containing an untrue imputation against the reputation of another'. The Defamation Act, 1961 does not provide a definition of *defamation*. However, a definition provided by the Irish courts in the 1970s is much favoured by lawyers. According to it, defamation is committed by the wrongful publication of a false statement about a person, which tends to lower that person in the eyes of right-thinking members of society or tends to hold that person up to hatred, ridicule or contempt, or causes that person to be shunned or avoided by right-thinking members of society.

It is of vital importance, therefore, that journalists should understand what material may, or may not be defamatory – or in other words, what constitutes an actionable libel. Newspapers, books, magazines, radio and television do not as a rule intentionally set out to publish or broadcast defamatory words; but pure inadvertence may easily result in a libel suit and heavy damages, as many publishers have found to their cost in court – not to mention the substantial sums handed over to plaintiffs in settlements reached before their actions even come on for trial.

The *intention* of the journalist writing or broadcasting the defamatory material has no relevance in the law of defamation. What matters is whether a reasonable person, reading the article, or seeing or listening to the telecast or broadcast, would tend to think less of the individual referred to in the alleged defamatory material or, to put it another way, whether it tends to hold him or her up to hatred, ridicule or contempt, or causes that person to be shunned or avoided by right-thinking members of society generally.

THE TEST

The test of whether a given statement contains a defamatory imputation or meaning is an objective one. It is the 'reasonable person' test – whether a reasonable person reading the printed words or listening to the broadcasted words regarded the statement as being defamatory.

Who would be regarded as the 'reasonable person'? A Circuit Court judge adjudicating over a libel action in his or her court decides all issues of law and fact. Therefore, that judge becomes the 'reasonable person' when deciding whether the words concerned were defamatory or capable of being defamatory. If the action was being heard in the High Court, the jury would be regarded as the 'reasonable person' because it is they who decide all issues of fact. Deciding whether the statement complained of was *capable* of being defamatory is a matter for the judge, but deciding whether the statement was in fact defamatory lies with the jury.

Curiously, this touches on one of the anomalies in this area of the law. If the plaintiff was seeking damages of up to £30,000 and therefore within the current jurisdiction of the Circuit Court, the action would be taken in that court, where a judge sits without a jury; whereas if the plaintiff was claiming damages in excess of £30,000 or unlimited damages, the action would be taken in the High Court. That limit of £30,000 will soon increase to £80,000. Under the Courts Act, 1988, juries were abolished in High Court personal injury actions but were retained for defamation actions.

A MATTER OF OPINION

The jury's function in defamation cases was emphasised by a Supreme Court judge in a noted libel action in the case of *Quigley v. Creation Ltd* in the early 1970s. That judicial pronouncement by the late Mr Justice Brian Walsh is as relevant today as it was thirty years ago, not only to explain the jury's role but also to enunciate the standard which the Supreme Court uses in considering whether it will set aside a jury's finding in libel actions. He stated: 'Basically, the question of libel or no libel is a matter of opinion, and opinions may vary reasonably within very wide limits. When a jury has found that there has been a libel, this court would be more slow to set aside such a verdict than in other types of actions and it would only do so if it was of opinion that the conclusions reached by the jury was one to which reasonable men could not or ought not to have come.'

To be defamatory, an imputation must tend to lower the plaintiff in the estimation of right-thinking members of society generally. Words are not defamatory, however much they may damage a person in the eyes of a section of the community, unless they also amount to disparagement of his reputation in the eyes of right-thinking people generally. The words are not defamatory if the standard of opinion of the particular section of the community is one which the courts cannot recognise or approve.

TRUTH AND LIBEL

In certain cases the truth of libellous matter, if it can be proved to the satisfaction of a court, may relieve the defendants of legal liability; but such justification is entirely a question of evidence and may be very difficult and costly to establish. Learning therefore to recognise a potentially libellous statement is of paramount importance.

THE ESSENCE OF LIBEL: DEFAMATION

No matter what time is left to the deadline for delivery of copy, the question the journalist must ask himself or herself is: 'Are these words capable of a defamatory meaning?' The journalist who suspects, deep down, that there may be a problem but says nothing and, instead, allows the copy through to the printers or permits the recorded tape to be broadcast or screened, is acting irresponsibly. If the question does arise, it is far better that it be decided or, at the very least, be discussed and brought to the attention of a superior prior to publication than later by a court with damages and costs the ultimate sanction. While the golden rule 'When in doubt, leave out' may seem a simplistic solution, strict observance of the rule could not, and should not, apply in every such situation. In practical terms, much will depend on the importance of the item and whether the publisher, perhaps after taking legal advice, wishes to assume the inherent risk to publish. The possibility or probability of handing out a large sum of money in damages and costs at the end of the day may not be the publisher's principal concern; the public interest duty to reveal a corruption in some public office, for example, may be more important to the publisher. That aside, the journalist who possesses an elementary knowledge of libel law will have a distinct advantage in recognising potentially troublesome copy and knowing how to cope with it.

ESSENTIAL ELEMENTS

There are three essential elements in every action for libel:

- the words complained of must refer to the plaintiff;
- the words must be published to a third party; and
- the words must be defamatory or capable of being defamatory.

Regarding the first of these, this is not always clear-cut. The plaintiff may not be named or identified in the specific publication. A journalist writing copy may decide not to name the subject, in the hope that because he or she is not naming names, as it were, the risk of being sued is therefore eliminated. That, however, is not sufficient. The subject of the item may be identifiable. Although not named, a plaintiff could produce evidence at a libel hearing from witnesses who could testify that they had read the offending article or listened to the broadcast complained of and had understood that it referred to the plaintiff. There have been numerous actions in which plaintiffs have proved this aspect of their case in this manner.

Regarding the second of these important elements, publication, it should be remembered that since reputation is one's estimation in the eyes of others, no defamation can occur without publication of the alleged defamatory words. Pride, self-respect and dignity may be affronted by a communication to the person defamed, but without publication to a third person there is no hurt to reputation and, therefore, no wrong of defamation. This distinguishes the tort of defamation from *criminal libel* (see pages 22, 23, 51, 77-80), for which there could be a prosecution without proof of publication to a third person. There is an amelioration for persons who are in the final stage of the distribution process of a libel, for example, newspaper vendors, newsagents and booksellers. Some cases decided over the years by the courts, both here and in Britain, have provided leniency in the rule regarding publication. If, as persons carrying on their business properly, they neither knew nor ought to have known that the newspaper or book contained a libel, they are not deemed to be publishers.

Regarding the third element, the meaning of the words complained of is probably the most important single factor in any libel action because it is from the meaning of the words that the defamation occurs. Crucially, the form of defence that the defendant will mount depends on whether the words complained of are statements of fact or expressions of opinion or comment and also the occasion on which the alleged defamatory statement was made, in other words, whether the occasion on which the alleged defamatory words were spoken was privileged in law.

INNUENDO

The law of defamation refers to the different meanings that may be given to words. There is (a) the ordinary and natural meaning and (b) the innuendo. In ordinary conversation, the word 'innuendo' is used by people to mean a statement made by way of hint or suggestion rather than directly. In defamation law, innuendo has a different meaning. The ordinary and natural meaning of words encompasses both the direct, literal meaning of the words and a meaning that can be inferred in those words.

In 1991, in a consultation paper on the civil law of defamation, the Law Reform Commission under the presidency of Mr Justice Ronan Keane, the present Chief Justice, by way of examples, explained the distinction in law between (a) the ordinary and natural meaning of words and (b) an innuendo. If it were said of a man that he was seen frequently entering a brothel, the words are regarded by the law as capable of being defamatory in their ordinary and natural meaning. If the statement is simply to the effect that the person was seen frequently entering a named premises, the words would not be regarded as capable of being defamatory in their ordinary and natural meaning. If, however, the named premises was a brothel, the statement is capable of containing a defamatory implication to anyone who knew that the house was a brothel but not to any one who did not.

In this latter instance, the words, although not defamatory in their ordinary and natural meaning, are capable of being defamatory by reason of an innuendo. The innuendo depends on proof by the plaintiff of extrinsic facts which demonstrate that a statement that is innocent on its face is defamatory.

A 1931 case from the English House of Lords, which every law student is familiar with, illustrates one of the clearest examples of a legal innuendo. Even the Law Reform Commission made detailed reference to it for this purpose in this paper. The facts of the case were that the defendants, by way of an advertisement for their chocolate product, issued a caricature of the plaintiff depicting him playing golf with a packet of their chocolate protruding from his pocket. Such a caricature was not defamatory *per se.* If the plaintiff were a professional golfer, there would have been nothing inconsistent with his status in his endorsing someone's products (by implication for reward). But the plaintiff was, in fact, an amateur golfer. The House of Lords held that the caricature was capable of bearing the meaning alleged in the legal innuendo and that was that the plaintiff had agreed to promote the defendant's products for reward and had thereby prostituted his reputation as an amateur golfer.

Because this area is at the very heart of the law of defamation, journalists are well advised to think very carefully and consider the weight that should be attached to every word they submit to print or utter for broadcasting.

GUIDELINES

It's not possible to legislate for every eventuality. Not even the wisest legal opinion would purport to be academically equipped to advise a publisher or journalist on how to eliminate risk in every article published or item broadcast. Knowing or identifying matter that is defamatory can be difficult, especially when a journalist is working to a deadline. A journalist working to a deadline in the 'pressure cooker' atmosphere of a newsroom is usually only concerned with operating to the dictat of a news or duty editor. Potential libels and other lurking dangers are far from the mind. But even in that situation, it is possible to take precautions to reduce that risk.

Simply put, when a journalist is preparing copy on a subject which falls into any of the following four categories, alarm bells should sound to put him or her on notice that extreme care should be exercised:

- words which impute unchastity or adultery to any person.
- words calculated to disparage in any office, profession, calling, trade or business.
- words imputing a criminal offence.
- words imputing a contagious disease.

The publication of defamatory words that fit into any of these categories is actionable without the plaintiff having to prove to a court that he or she suffered special damage as a result of the publication. They are used here as warning signs that should not be ignored.

Generally, any words that reflect adversely on the plaintiff's moral, intellectual or professional character may be libellous and may give rise to grounds for an action to be taken. As with every action commenced at law, each case is judged on its own merits. It should be remembered that a journalist's mistake is not a defence in a libel action. Nor is inadvertence an excuse.

It should be noted that what was regarded by a jury as defamatory ten, twenty or more years ago, might not necessarily be the case today, for the reason that public values change as society changes.

Hatred, ridicule and contempt   The Civil Bill (the originating document in a Circuit Court action) or the Statement of Claim served by the plaintiff on the defendant in a High Court action for libel or an Affidavit grounding an application for an injunction to stop the publication of an allegedly defamatory matter will contain a paragraph something like the following:

> As a result of the said publication, the plaintiff has been greatly injured in his credit and reputation and in his office as aforesaid and has been brought into public odium, hatred, ridicule and contempt.

The wording of the legal document will depend on the circumstances of the particular case but certainly the words 'hatred', 'ridicule' and 'contempt' will usually be included in all cases of libel by the barrister drafting the document. On the face of it, the definition is an extremely wide one, giving a plaintiff latitude to issue a writ for libel if an unkind word is published against him or her. However, for the comfort of the journalist who sees himself or herself

harassed by restrictive libel law, the law does allow considerable latitude of comment to the Press, as will become apparent when we consider the various defences available to the publisher.

A working knowledge of the law of libel is essential for all journalists and will enable an editor to gauge any risk being taken in publishing questionable copy. The Irish are an extremely litigious race and, with such heavy, indeed swingeing, damages being awarded in courts in recent times, not to mention punishing costs, the days of 'Publish and be damned' are the exception rather than the norm.

DEFAMATORY IMPUTATIONS

One of the difficulties in advising on this aspect of the law is that it is not possible to say with certainty that any particular imputation is defamatory. In addition, the question whether any imputation is defamatory is not a matter of law, but a matter of fact for the jury, and no jury will necessarily reach the same decision as another. It may be helpful to mention some previous decisions of the courts both in this country and in England in determining whether particular words are capable of conveying a defamatory imputation.

In the recent past, it has been held defamatory to publish that a plaintiff secured a licence for a radio station in circumstances which gave rise to a suspicion of bribery or corrupt practices, or that the plaintiff had engaged in corrupt practices which warranted investigation by the Flood Tribunal, or that a plaintiff was involved in or tolerated serious crime, or that a plaintiff personally supported anti-semitism and violent communist oppression, or that a government minister had refused to disclose to Gardaí the names of two alleged child abusers, or that a barrister was a sympathiser with terrorist causes.

It has also been held defamatory to publish of someone that he has falsely accused another of some criminal offence, or that he has cheated at horse-racing or at cards, or that he has been blackballed on seeking admission to a club, or that he has entertained with a view to winning money from his guests by gaming, or that he is not a proper person to be received in society. A suggestion made by an auctioneer that the plaintiff had not acted in accordance with the high traditions of his profession as a solicitor was accepted as being defamatory. Imputations of sexual impropriety made against the plaintiffs in a book were held to be defamatory. To impute that the plaintiff made deliberate false statements to a local corporation for the purpose of deceiving the corporation, and that the plaintiff was unfit for public office was also held to be defamatory. To accuse a person wrongfully of theft is defamatory. It was held libellous and actionable to say that a man was a bigot in religious matters. It has been held defamatory to write that a man had been guilty of a breach of duty, or that he was dishonest, or indiscreet, or that he was a communist.

Hundreds of decided cases could be quoted here as examples of defamatory imputations but whether or not an imputation is defamatory will vary with time, place and the state of public opinion.

Vulgar abuse   Vulgar abuse is defined as the reviling of a person in terms which are common, crude, uncouth, rude, coarse or in bad taste. It has always been accepted that vulgar abuse of a person is not defamatory but, while this is largely true, no such rule exists and journalists should be wary.

Malice   Malice is not an essential element of a libel. Even where there has been an absence of ill-will or spite or of libellous intention, damages may be awarded. The most innocent-looking words may be held defamatory if they fail the 'reasonable person' test in the minds of a High Court jury or of a judge in the Circuit Court (see pp 14f)

LIBEL ON CORPORATE BODIES

Corporate bodies may defend their good name in court. The libel must reflect on the conduct of the corporation as such, not just on the individuals composing it. There was a recent example of this when a Dublin bank obtained libel damages and an injunction against an individual who had picketed the bank with a placard containing a defamatory statement about the bank.

In a general way, newspapers, magazines and current affairs programmes on radio and TV are free to criticize public bodies and, unless corruption is alleged, there is no great risk of a libel action being taken.

Similarly, provided no corrupt motive is alleged, the decisions of judges and the behaviour of the Gardaí and other public officials may be criticised. But as regards judges and the courts, prudence must be observed for fear of the contempt laws (see Chapter 4).

VICARIOUS LIABILITY

A question frequently asked by journalists relates to whether they, as individuals, can be directly sued by a defendant in a libel action, rather than the newspaper, book or magazine publisher, radio or television station. We are not concerned here with printers, booksellers or newsvendors.

It is a general principle at common law that any person who publishes a defamatory statement is liable to the plaintiff. The individual defendant in a tort action is not infrequently 'a man of straw' and there is an old legal mechanism that enables a plaintiff to fix responsibility on someone other than the impecunious journalist. That is the principle of vicarious liability in which one person is liable for the wrong committed by another; the master is liable for the wrongs of his servant but only for those wrongs which arise out of or are within the scope of the servant's employment. In determining if a person is a servant of the employer (publisher), the question is paramount as to whether there is the necessary element of control by the master over the servant. Was the relationship between the journalist and his or her publisher sufficient to make the defendant vicariously liable for the wrong done?

In the case of an employee journalist, the issue is clear. Equally, in the case of a freelance journalist who, for example, submitted an article or item to the newspaper or radio station for publication or broadcast, the matter is also clear. In both situations, the publisher becomes liable for their torts. At common law, any person who publishes a defamatory statement is liable to the plaintiff. As a consequence, the journalist who wrote or broadcast the offending piece could be joined as a defendant and especially so if the matter was published under his or her name. However, generally, the journalist is not joined. That should not in any way relieve the journalist from the obligation of acting with total responsibility.

LIMITATION PERIODS

As the law stands, an action for damages for libel must be taken within six years from the date on which the cause of action accrued. This is an exceedingly long limitation period from the perspective of both plaintiffs and defendants. On the other hand, an action for damages for slander must be brought within three years from the date on which the cause of action accrued.

CRIMINAL LIBEL

Apart from the civil tort of defamation, newspapers can be prosecuted on a criminal charge for publishing a defamatory libel. The Defamation Act mentions only newspapers in this context. Criminal proceedings may be taken by private as well as by public prosecutors, but no criminal prosecution can be commenced against any proprietor, publisher, editor or any person responsible for the publication of a newspaper for any libel published, without an order being first obtained from a judge of the High Court. That application must be held *in camera.*

Part II of the Defamation Act, 1961 sets out the procedures for commencing and prosecuting criminal libel in addition to laying out the maximum monetary fine and prison sentence that can be imposed on conviction, depending on whether the prosecution is tried by the District Court or by a judge and jury. The ancestry for this form of prosecution has its origin in the Newspaper Libel and Registration Act, 1881. Section 8 of the 1961 Act stipulates that notice of the original application is given to the person accused. He or she has the right to be heard before leave to commence the prosecution is granted. The Act provides for the charge to be tried on indictment by a judge and jury but it also provides circumstances where it may be tried summarily by the District Court.

So far as it can be ascertained, there have been only three applications in this country for leave to commence such prosecutions. Since the 1961 Act came into force, all have been refused. Two of them related to criminal libel and the most recent, in October 1996, related to blasphemous libel, an offence that has its origins in Article 40, section 6 (1) of the Constitution. This states: 'The publication or utterance of blasphemous, seditious or indecent matter is an offence which shall punishable in accordance with law.'

The principles laid down by the High Court for the granting of leave to institute a prosecution are:

(a) Firstly, the applicant must establish a clear *prima facie* case in the sense that it is a case which is so clear at first sight that there is beyond argument a case to answer if the matter goes before a criminal court.
(b) The libel must be a serious one, so serious that it is proper for the criminal law to be invoked.
(c) Although it may be a relevant factor that the libel is unusually likely to provoke a breach of the peace, that is not a necessary ingredient.
(d) The question of the public interest must be taken into account on the basis that the judge should ask himself the question: Does the public interest *require* the institution of criminal proceedings?

2

Defending a libel action

A writ for libel is rarely issued without an initial contact between the plaintiff individually or, more likely, the plaintiff's solicitor and the publisher. The vast majority of claims are settled out of court during the course of pre-liminary negotiations between the parties. By and large, initial contact is made by way of a solicitor's letter to the proprietors, and usually to the editor as well, drawing attention to the alleged libel and demanding a retraction or apology and, perhaps, compensation in the form of the payment of a sum of money.

Consideration must then be given to the question whether it would be more prudent to retreat into the position of offering the apology and a cash payment to cover agreed damages and costs, rather than to fight. Delay in making a decision at this stage may prove very expensive later. Sometimes, all a plaintiff may be seeking is a clarification or an apology and, if that is met, no action may ensue. Depending on the exact circumstances of the case, the publisher might be left with no alternative but to allow the matter to proceed to court, ignoring the demand for an apology and compensation. Of course, if an apology is published, an action may still go ahead with the pub-lisher seeking to mitigate his loss by pointing to the publication of the apology as evidence of his or her desire to correct the damage allegedly caused by the original publication.

THE MEMO

After a quick check by the editor, usually with the relevant news editor or duty editor, regarding the substance of the complaint, it is left to the news editor or other executive to establish the *bona fides* of the complaint. If it appears that the alleged libel originated in the work of a journalist, the individual concerned will be asked to write a memorandum, setting out, in as much detail as possible, the background to the publication of the matter complained of and other relevant detail.

PUBLISHING AN APOLOGY

When the dust settles after the initial investigation and it transpires that there was substance to the complaint resulting in some wrong (no matter to what degree) the question which must be addressed is whether an apology should be published. While the publisher may wish to exercise his prerogative and not offer an apology, experience has shown that there is little to be gained from adopting that stand. If a member of the public has been defamed, it is only right and just that that person's character should be vindicated as soon as possible after the damage was caused. Should the publisher fail to publish an apology, or delay in doing so until the die is well and truly cast, almost certainly the award of damages will be greater than it otherwise would be.

The practice of publishing corrections and clarifications as a matter of daily practice has much to commend it, not least because it may sway those affected from issuing proceedings.

Section 17 of the Defamation Act deals with the question of apologies. It states: 'In any action for defamation, it shall be lawful for the defendant (after notice in writing of his intention so to do, duly given to the plaintiff at the time of filing or delivering the plea in the action) to give evidence, in mitigation of damage, that he made or offered an apology to the plaintiff for such defamation before the commencement of the action, or as soon afterwards as he had an opportunity of doing so, in case the action shall have been commenced before there was an opportunity of making or offering such apology.'

This is saying, in effect, that the defendant may give evidence to the court that he offered an apology to the defendant before the proceedings were commenced or as soon as he had an opportunity to do so. The legislation clearly recognises that this evidence may be given in order to reduce the damages against the defendant. By failing to give the apology, the defendant is not helping his own cause; and by delaying in publishing an apology he is aggravating the libel to an extent that may be used by the plaintiff to receive even greater damages later.

Whatever the rights or wrongs of the alleged libellous matter of which complaint is made, section 17 puts the newspaper, magazine, broadcasting station or whatever publisher is involved into a Catch 22 situation. In reality, if an apology is published in the first instance, guilt is being admitted at a very early stage, and the only question remaining is the amount of compensation that the plaintiff should recover. However, if the apology is not published or is delayed, the legislation is there to be used against the publisher at the hearing.

Given that the publication of an apology can have a significant bearing on the final outcome of the action at a much later time, it is absolutely essential that legal advice should be obtained before one is published. One of the main reasons for this is that a decision like this is made to some extent in the 'dark'. Almost certainly the publisher will not have all the information that would ultimately be available by the time the action comes to hearing and will have to 'second-guess' the outcome of the action. If a complaint is mishandled, the eventual outcome of the case could be very severe in terms of a high, or higher, award of damages than might otherwise be the case. The legal adviser should be consulted the moment a claim is received .

A second reason for this is that the actual wording of the apology is crucial. While a plaintiff's legal advisers will put forward their specific form of the apology in terms that will suit the plaintiff best, the publisher is equally entitled to an input. Forms of apology drafted by lawyers for plaintiffs are usually worded in such a way that if they were published without amendment by the publisher, they could be later used at the hearing as evidence of the admission that a libel had been committed, and as evidence also that the publisher had accepted and admitted that the plaintiff had suffered. Nothing, of course, should be admitted by the publisher which he might wish to contest later.

Yet a further reason for this is that there may be cases where an apology should not be published at all. The publication of an apology in the wrong circumstances could serve as an encouragement to a claimant who may perceive the making of an apology as an admission of liability. Equally, the publisher could be making a lot of trouble for himself in a situation where he may wish to stand over or justify at the trial what was published as being the truth. When a publisher decides, however, that no apology should be made, he should feel, after taking professional advice, that he had very strong grounds for defending the action.

LODGING MONEY WITH THE DEFENCE

Publishers are placed in a dilemma by the Rules of the Superior Courts which provide at Order 22, rule 1, sub-rule 3: 'In actions for libel or slander ... money may not be paid into Court under this rule unless liability is admitted in the defence.' This provision, which is confined to defamation actions, effectively precludes publishers from lodging money in court unless the publisher is admitting fault.

As a consequence of this rule the defendant publisher is denied the relief available to defendants in, for example, other tort actions and in contract disputes. It should be explained that when a defendant lodges an amount of money with the defence and it transpires that the judge awards the plaintiff a sum of money which is less than the amount lodged by the defendant, the plaintiff must pay the full costs which arise from the date of the lodgment to the date of the judgment. That would constitute the greater portion of the costs and would include the full trial costs. The judge, of course, is unaware of the amount lodged with the defence until after his ruling.

The jury is never informed if money is lodged. This is stipulated in Order 22, rule 7 which states, in part: 'Where an action is tried by judge and jury, no communication either of the fact that money has been paid into court or of the amount thereof, shall be made to the jury.'

UNINTENTIONAL DEFAMATION: OFFER OF AMENDS

Section 21 of the 1961 Act provides that a person who unintentionally defames another person may make an offer of amends, including the publication of a suitable correction of the words complained of and 'a sufficient apology'. If the offer is accepted and is duly performed, no proceedings shall be taken against the person making the offer in respect of the publication in question. But if the offer is not accepted, then the publisher/defendant may use the evidence of the offer and the fact that the matter was published innocently by him as a defence. However, in order to avail of this defence, the publisher must, among other things, be able to prove that he exercised all reasonable care in relation to the publication.

THE SOURCE OF THE LIBEL

Other journalists involved in processing the particular copy may also be asked to write memos. Usually, the personnel concerned will be working from memory in detailing accounts of what transpired as they handled the copy at successive stages. While it will normally become apparent early in the investigation where the problem arose, all too often it emerges that it originated with the journalist in the first instance 'taking a chance' that the story or item was fine for publication or through inadvertence or, indeed, through 'picking-up' a story from a colleague. Fortunes have been handed away in damages through a sub-editor's carelessness or lack of attention to detail when reducing or re-writing the submitted copy through bad punctuation and writing up misleading headings. The history of libel actions has also taught journalists and newspaper lawyers that the editorial office has been a fertile source of grounds for action. A word, a sentence or a paragraph dropped from a story can drastically alter the original story to create a dangerous imbalance which could give rise to a cause of action.

NOTEBOOKS

Newspapers and other publications would be advised to issue reporting staff with notebooks which should be retained, duly dated, for at least twelve months. One needs to bear in mind that a plaintiff has six years in which to take a libel action. Freelance journalists could be similarly instructed. If such a course were adopted and checked from time to time to see that it was being observed, the task of proprietors, editors and those charged with checking complaints would be simplified.

The one disadvantage of retaining notebooks is that they would form part of the material that would be handed to the plaintiffs side prior to the hearing should they be granted an order of discovery by the court, given that the notes were prepared in the first instance when the libel proceedings were not in contemplation. Nevertheless, the advantages considerably outweigh the disadvantages in practical terms and, on balance, notebooks should be kept.

THE CASE FOR THE DEFENCE

Assuming that the plaintiff succeeds on the balance of probabilities in establishing that the words complained of referred to him, that they were published to a third party and that they were defamatory or capable of being defamatory, it is then for the defence to consider its case. There are a number of legal defences open to the publishers.

The principal defences to an action for damages for libel are:

- justification
- privilege
- fair comment

- apology
- accord and satisfaction
- consent.

Of these, justification, privilege (absolute and qualified) and fair comment are the principal ones.

Justification is the defence of truth. Once the plaintiff has shown the matter complained of to be defamatory, the law presumes the statement to be false. Thus, the burden of proof is on the defendant to establish the truth of the statement if the defence raised is that of justification. It is a good defence to a claim for libel to prove that the words complained of are true in substance and in fact. It does not apply to a situation where the alleged defamatory meaning relates to comment or opinion, such as an editorial. But the proof required to establish such a plea is very strict, with the burden of proving the truth of the statement resting on the defendant. If the defendant fails to establish this plea, the consequence could be a sanction in the form of heavier damages for aggravating the damage caused in the first place.

On a further cautionary note, a publisher relying on the plea of *justification* will plan on producing evidence from witnesses to prove the truth of the alleged defamatory statement. If a reporter had based a story or article on information supplied by a source, who wished to remain anonymous, the publisher would be at a considerable disadvantage in seeking to establish the truth of the piece because the anonymous source could not be called as a witness. That is why much thought and consideration must be given to preparing such a defence.

The successful defence of justification mounted by RTE to the libel claim brought in the Cooper-Flynn case resulted in the action taking a full 28 days at the end of which the jury found that RTE had proved that the plaintiff advised or encouraged other named persons to evade tax. However, the defendants did not prove to the satisfaction of the jury that the plaintiff had induced the third defendant to evade paying his tax.

The questions put to the jury in the 'issue paper' in that case are reproduced here to show the complex nature of the issues that juries in libel actions are often faced with, especially in cases where the defendant pleads justification of the matter complained of.

1. Have the defendants proved that the plaintiff induced the third named defendant to evade his lawful obligation to pay tax by not availing of the tax amnesty?

If the answer is 'no', proceed to question 2.
If the answer is 'yes', proceed to no further.
[The jury answered 'no'.]

2. Have the defendants proved that the plaintiff advised or encouraged other persons – being those referred to in the evidence – to evade tax? If the answer is 'no', proceed to question 4 to assess damages. if the answer is 'yes', proceed to question 3.
   [The jury answered 'yes'.]

3. In view of the finding to question 2, has the plaintiff's reputation suffered material injury by reason of the matters published relating to the third named defendant?
   [The jury answered 'no'.]

4. If the answer to questions 1 and 2 is 'no', assess damages under the heading (a) general damages, (b) aggravation of such damages.

5. If the answer to question 1 is 'no', and 2 and 3 are 'yes', assess damages to the material injury to the plaintiff's reputation.
   [The jury answer 'none' when directed to give a written response to this question.]

At the time of going to print the case was under appeal to the Supreme Court.

PRIVILEGE

There are two kinds of privilege, absolute and qualified. Absolute privilege applies principally in the case of reports of the Oireachtas, to committees of the Oireachtas and to the courts. Insofar as journalists are concerned, section 18 (1) of the Defamation Act states that fair and accurate reports of court proceedings publicly heard in the State or in Northern Ireland, if published contemporaneously, are privileged. This is dealt with more fully in Chapter 3.

Qualified privilege is offered to certain newspaper and broadcast reports by section 24 of the Defamation Act (see second schedule of the Act). The one element which destroys privilege is *malice*. Malice, in law, is any wrong or improper motive, but it need hardly be added that malice is a stranger to the vocabulary of the *bona fide* journalist.

The second schedule to the Defamation Act should be read and digested, but a word of explanation is necessary in order to fully understand what reports have qualified privilege.

Part One of the second schedule sets out four categories of reports which qualify for this privilege. They include reports from a house of the legislature of any foreign State; reports of an international organisation or conference of which Ireland is a member or to which Ireland sends a representative; reports of an international court of justice or other tribunal deciding matters in dispute between states; court proceedings in foreign courts; and fair and accurate copies of extracts from a public registry. All of these are given qualified privilege *provided* they are fair and accurate and the proceedings to which the report relates were heard in public. However, the privilege attaches to proceedings in foreign courts even if they are not heard in public.

Part Two of the second schedule sets out a long list of statements which are privileged 'subject to explanation or contradiction'. To understand the meaning of the words quoted above reference must be made to section 24 (2) of the Defamation Act. Paraphrased, the sub-section states that these statements have qualified privilege only if it is proved in a libel action that the defendant has been requested by a defendant to publish in the newspaper or to broadcast from the broadcasting station from which the original broadcast was made a reasonable statement by way of explanation or contradiction, and has refused or neglected to do so, or has done so in a manner not adequate or not reasonable having regard to all the circumstances.

REPORT V. COMMENT

Strictly speaking, only reports are privileged. It is, therefore, essential to distinguish between report and comment. A *report* is an account, abbreviated or otherwise, of proceedings. On the other hand, *comment* is the judgment or opinion of the journalist on these proceedings.

Whether journalists are engaged in reporting court or parliamentary proceedings, Bord Pleanála hearings, meetings of local authorities or any of the meetings or hearings given or deemed to be given qualified privilege in the second schedule of the 1961 Act, they should bear in mind the distinction between report and comment: if privilege is to be claimed in respect of fair and accurate reports, report and comment must be kept separate and distinct. No privilege can be claimed for comment, as distinct from strict reporting. Reporters should avoid editorializing in this context.

FAIR COMMENT

Fair comment does not negative defamation but it establishes a defence to an action founded on defamation. The defence that the words complained of are a fair comment on a matter of public interest means that the words, although libellous, are not actionable.

Although it is primarily a matter for the newspaper's legal advisers to consider, both before and during the heat of a libel battle, journalists would be well advised to remember that comment may be no less damaging than strict reporting and that the law of libel does not allow a publisher and his journalistic employees unbridled expression of opinion. The matter commented upon must be of public interest and the comment or opinion must be fair in the sense of being honestly held and acceptable to a fair-minded person.

What is and is not a matter of public interest is a question of law for the judge to decide. It is self-explanatory in the sense that it relates to public rather than private matters, such as comment on education, sporting, cultural and scientific matters as well as local and national issues.

THE INDIVIDUAL'S RIGHT TO BE HEARD

One of the principles of natural justice affords journalists a beacon to follow in seeking to strike a sense of balance and fairness. That principle is *audi alteram partem* – the right to be heard. Lawyers speak of natural and constitutional justice in relation to the fairness of procedures, which must be observed by tribunals, government ministers and others. The superior courts have condemned decisions that denied that fundamental right. Journalists, no less than public officials, are charged with the obligation of acting fairly. In no sense can a report be described as fair and balanced if the journalist chooses to ignore the right of an individual to give his side of the story or to answer an allegation made against him.

All too frequently, libel writs have been issued by individuals who were not contacted before the journalist went into print or went on air with an item of news or, worse still, a piece of gossip or rumour taken on the word of a so-called reliable source. Experience has taught that most often it is not the big expose stories which have landed publishers in hot water but the small, social-type items to which the same degree of care must be given as the 'hard news' story.

The following may be of assistance in helping journalists to steer clear of trouble:

- Don't be economical with the truth. If journalists have a doubt about a story, the matter should be discussed and, if necessary, legal advice obtained. The best defence the journalist will have is to be able to stand over what is reported, without equivocation, and to be able to demonstrate that every effort was made to get both sides of the story.
- Do not trivialise potentially serious stories, either in the content of the copy or in the make-up of the headline. Both can easily distort the factual report and misrepresent to a dangerous degree the motive of the people involved.
- Greater control should be exercised over copy prior to publication.
- The advent of new technology, involving on-screen subbing and layout, means that the reporter's copy undergoes several changes prior to publication. Thought should be given to retaining what is known in print as 'hard-copy' or a true record of the original material as it left the hands of the reporter in the first instance.
- Avoid using rumour or hearsay.
- Facts are sacred and they should be checked to ensure that they could be proved to be facts. Independent verification should be sought, if possible.
- Journalists should be libel conscious, i.e. they should be conscious at all times of the threat of libel.
- Photo-journalists and newsroom personnel should ensure that the people whose photographs are to be published are correctly identified in the accompanying captions.
- The subject of critical opinions should be afforded the right to reply.
- Check that the headline accurately reflects the story and is not itself libellous (the juxtapositioning of the word 'disgrace' beside a photograph of a GAA official was held to be defamatory by a Circuit Court judge in 1999. There was no reference to the word 'disgrace' in the body of the accompanying newspaper article).

On-line publishing is part of the phenomenal growth in Internet and e-mail technology. However, hand-in-hand with this development is the question of the employer's liability for the publication of defamatory matter on the

Internet. The same essential elements apply in this form of defamation as examined earlier. In an employer/employee situation, if something defamatory is published on the Internet, proceedings can be taken against the author of the material, the author's employer or both. Again, as discussed above, the basis for such a suit is that the employer was vicariously liable for the tort of the employee.

This country's first Internet prosecution arose in early 2000 when a young man was sentenced to two-and-a-half years' imprisonment for sending messages to bulletin sites and by e-mail, falsely and maliciously accusing a teacher in his former school of paedophile activities and of sexually abusing pupils.

The Non-Fatal Offences against the Person Act, 1997 was utilised by the Gardaí for the purposes of a prosecution which arose out of the publication by a Co. Mayo businessman of an advertisement on the Internet of a woman as a prostitute willing to perform various sexual acts. The woman whose mobile telephone number was supplied in the advertisement was a competitor of the accused. Evidence was given at the Circuit Court that the woman received more than one hundred calls in the two days after it was first published. Although initially denying that he had placed the advertisement which he titled 'Exclusive.Maureen' the accused later admitted the offence to Gardaí. An offer by the accused to pay his victim £10,000 by way of compensation was rejected by the judge who said that amount was totally inadequate and would not come near what a civil remedy for the case would amount to in an award of damages. The accused was put back for sentence when the Court applied the Probation Act after being told that the accused had paid 'substantial compensation' to the victim (see *Irish Times*, 19 May 2001).

This particular provision of the 1961 Act states that every person who maliciously publishes any defamatory libel, knowing the same to be false, shall, on conviction, he liable to a fine not exceeding £200 or to imprisonment for a term not exceeding one year or to both such fine and imprisonment.

The High Court in London ordered a disgruntled former employee who made false accusations, against an executive in his former employer in a series of e-mails to pay £26,000 damages and costs estimated at £100,000. The culprit, who used a false name, denied writing the e-mails but the judge ruled against him. Disclosure orders were made during the course of the investigation against Internet Service Provider CompuSave and Microsoft to compel them to disclose account information.

In the US, Online anonymity campaigners suffered a set back when a Florida court ruled that ISPs could be compelled by the courts to identify people who post defamatory messages on internal bulletin boards.

DAMAGES

The Defamation Act does not contain any provision allowing a judge to give guidance to a jury on the amount of damages they might consider assessing in any particular case. Within the past few years, there have been jury awards of £300,000 and £250,000 in libel cases. The Supreme Court upheld the first of these but in October 2000, after comparing the awards in both of these cases, it set aside the latter award as being disproportionately high and directed a retrial on the question of damages only. The general principle applied by the Supreme Court in considering the jury assessment of damages is that stated by a Supreme Court judge in another libel action appeal: 'a fundamental principle of the law of compensatory damages is that the award must always be reasonable and fair and bear due correspondence with the injury suffered. In my view, the sum awarded in this case went far beyond what a reasonable jury applying the law to all the relevant considerations could reasonably have awarded. It was so disproportionately high that in my view it should not be allowed to stand.'

The Supreme Court, in dealing with the £300,000 award in *O'Brien v Mirror Group Newspapers & Others* (25 October 2000), disapproved of a 1996 decision of the English Court of Appeal that guidance should be given by the trial judge to the jury on the assessment of damages in the form of comparison with precedent awards in both personal injury and libel cases and to the purchasing power of a particular award as well as to the level of awards suggested by counsel and the judge himself or herself. In a minority judgment one of the Supreme Court judges expressed the view that such guidance should be given to High Court juries.

Up to the present, the Supreme Court has not exercised its power to substitute for the sum awarded by the High Court in defamation cases such sum that the court thinks appropriate.

Article 40.6.1.i of the Constitution guarantees freedom of expression. So does the European Convention on Human Rights and Fundamental Freedoms which states at Article 10:

1. Everyone has the right to freedom of expression. This shall include freedom to hold opinions and to receive and impart information and ideas without reference to public authority and regardless of frontiers. This Article shall not prevent States from requiring the licensing of broadcasting, television or cinema enterprises.
2. The exercise of these freedoms, since it carries with it duties and responsibilities, may be subject to such formalities, conditions, restrictions or penalties as are prescribed by law and necessary in a demo-

cratic society, in the interests of national security, territorial integrity or
public safety, for the prevention of disorder or crime, for the protection
of health or morals, for the protection of the reputation or rights of
others, for preventing the disclosure of information received in confidence, or for maintaining the authority and impartiality of the judiciary.

It is arguable that the rights protected by Article 10 of the Convention, i.e. the
right to communicate, the right to information and the right to freedom of
expression, are, for the most part, rights protected by Article 40.3.1 and
Article 40.6.1.i of the Constitution. The rights guaranteed in both the Constitution and the Convention are not absolute. An appropriate balance must
be achieved in terms, for example, of protecting a person's reputation.
Already, the Strasbourg-based European Court of Human Rights has held
that an award of libel damages in an English case was in breach of Article 10
of the Convention because of a lack of adequate and effective safeguards
against disproportionality in the national law of England and Wales.

   While the Supreme Court recently declined to reform the common law to
enable guidance to be given to libel juries in assessing the level of damages
to a plaintiff, a complaint against Ireland in the European Court of Human
Rights alleging a violation of Article 10 of the Convention is a possibility.

   In *De Rossa v. Independent Newspaper Plc* (30 July 1999) the Supreme
Court ruled that the assessment of damages in a defamation action in the
High Court was a matter for the jury who should base their assessment
entirely on the facts as found by them. Figures awarded in other cases based
on different facts were not matters which the jury was entitled to take into
account, it said.

   The other findings by the court in that case are equally important.
According to the official *Irish Reports* of the judgments, the court held that it
was not necessarily fair to compare awards for damages for loss of reputation
to damages for personal injury, as compensation by damages for loss of
reputation operated as a vindication of the plaintiff to the public and as
consolation to the plaintiff for a wrong done and not as a monetary recom-
pense for harm which was measurable in money. It also held that if the judge
and counsel could mention figures to the jury, the proceedings would be in
danger of developing into an auction; if comparison with previous libel and
personal injury awards were made, the jury would be overwhelmed with
figures. Such a practice would lead to confusion. Accordingly, in assessing
the *quantum* (amount) of an award, the jury could not be given guidelines by
the court or by counsel in relation to the appropriate level of damages
awarded in personal injury actions or other defamation actions.

INJUNCTIONS

The granting of an injunction to restrain publication in a defamation case is rare. The reason the Law Reform Commission gave for this is that courts do not wish to impose prior restraints on free speech and they are reluctant to usurp in advance the function of the court which will eventually try the case. However, since that statement was made in 1991, such an injunction was granted. From the judgment in that case, *Reynolds v. Elio Malocco trading as 'Patrick' and others*, in December 1998, the following principles emerge:

(1) A plaintiff in such an action in order to obtain an interlocutory (or continuing injunction) must show not merely that he has raised a serious issue concerning the words complained of but that there is no doubt but that the words are defamatory.
(2) In addition, if the defendant intends to plead justification or any other recognised defence, normally an injunction of this type will be refused.

However, this was not a 'normal' case. Having found that the words complained of were defamatory of the plaintiff, the High Court judge (Peter Kelly J) decided that it was open to the court to examine the evidence adduced by the defendant in support of the plea of justification he was putting forward in order to ascertain whether the plea had 'any substance or prospect of success'. Having done so, the judge concluded that the evidence put forward to support the plea of justification did not go anywhere near demonstrating the existence of an arguable prospect of making out the defence of justification. The plaintiff had made out a sufficiently strong case to satisfy the test required for the granting of an interlocutory injunction.

In addition, while also satisfied that his discretion must be exercised in favour of granting an injunction rather than refusing it, the judge added: 'To refuse it would be to consign the plaintiff to a trial where damages would be an inadequate remedy because of the virtual impossibility of ever recovering any sum awarded.'

3

Court reporting

One of the greatest sources of danger as far as the law of libel is concerned is the court of law. In this country, there is an abundance of courts, which provide newspapers, magazines, radio and TV with a plentiful supply of copy on a daily basis. The various courts are:

- The District Court – civil and criminal
- The Circuit Court – civil and criminal
- The High Court – civil
- The Central Criminal Court – criminal
- The Special Criminal Court – criminal
- The Court of Criminal Appeal – criminal
- The Supreme Court – civil but has jurisdiction to hear criminal appeals from the Central Criminal Court (High Court).

Add to these other types of hearings of a judicial nature such as, for example, Employment Appeal Tribunals and Army courts martial, and the source becomes even wider. By the very nature of court cases defamatory things will be said and reporting of them is only permissible because of the privilege accorded by the Defamation Act.

Section 18 (1) of the Act states:

> A fair and accurate report published in any newspaper or broadcast by means of wireless telegraphy as part of any programme or service provided by means of a broadcasting station within the State or in Northern Ireland of proceedings publicly heard before any court established by law and exercising judicial authority within the State or in Northern Ireland shall, if published or broadcast contemporaneously with such proceedings, be privileged.

Section 18 (2) states: 'Nothing in subsection (1) of this section shall authorise the publication or broadcasting of any blasphemous or obscene matter.'

Regarding subsection (1) certain words should be emphasised: 'fair', 'accurate' and 'contemporaneously'. To be given the mantle of privilege or immunity from being sued for libel, the report (note: not comment) of the case must be *fair* and it must be *accurate*. It must have been *publicly* heard and it must be published *contemporaneously*. This latter word would seem to mean that the report should be published in the next available edition or bulletin to get the protection of privilege.

'Publicly heard' in subsection (1) is also extremely important. Many reporters have experience of being present in court when the judge made an order to exclude the public or persons not directly concerned with the case. An example of this is to be found in section 16 (2) of the Criminal Procedure Act, 1967. This states:

> Where the court is satisfied, because of the nature or circumstances of the case or otherwise in the interests of justice, that it is desirable, the court may exclude the public or any particular portion of the public or any particular person or persons except *bona fide* representatives of the Press from the court during the hearing.

The fact that the reporter is allowed to remain present and to fulfil his function would not, *per se,* limit his or her right to statutory privilege. However, if a judge, for a reason best known to himself or herself, rules that a certain case be held *in camera* and excludes the public, including the Press, from the hearing, the journalist who subsequently compiles a report by reference to the documents on file or in the possession of either party to the litigation or by getting an abbreviated version of the hearing from one or all of the parties, is treading on dangerous ground. Not alone would privilege not attach to such a report, but the reporter and the organ which published it would face proceedings for contempt of court with fines, prison sentences and sequestration of assets as possible sanctions.

When a judge makes a ruling to hold a case *in camera* it must be obeyed. The matter is too grave for any one reporter to risk the ire of the bench for the sake of a story. However, occasions have arisen and, no doubt, will arise where such rulings have been questioned, but it must be done in a proper manner by legal representatives acting on behalf of the publisher, who will go before the judge in question or to a higher court on appeal to argue why the case should be heard in public. (See judgment of the Supreme Court, dated 2 April 1998 in the following two sets of proceedings heard as one: *Irish Times Ltd, Independent Newspapers (Ireland) Ltd, News Group Newspapers Ltd v. Judge Anthony G. Murphy; and RTE v. Ireland, the Attorney General and Judge Anthony G. Murphy*, in which the court unanimously upheld a challenge to a ban on contemporaneous reporting of a criminal trial in Cork, that the constitutional requirement that justice should be administered in public should be adhered to, except in exceptional circumstances, and that impeding media access to courts was equivalent to limiting public access. It ruled that a ban on such reporting should only be issued where there was a real risk of prejudicing the defendant's right to a fair trial that could not be avoided by rulings or directions given by the trial judge.)

A HEARING 'IN CHAMBERS'

This term sometimes appears in legislation. It could mean that the hearing will be held 'in private,' 'otherwise than in public,' or '*in camera.*' However, it is considered here in a different context. Occasionally a judge will decide to hear a case in chambers, that is, his or her own private office in the court building. The publication of a report of what occurs in chambers, garnered from the legal representatives present would not be protected by privilege because they fall foul of s.18 (1) of the Defamation Act which specifically uses the word '**publicly heard.**'

However, the fact that the hearing is being held in chambers may be as a matter of convenience such as the unavailability of a court building or after normal court hours. In any case, it would be open to the presiding judge to declare that such a sitting is a public sitting and this would have the effect not only of permitting the particular issue before the court to be reported but of giving the reporter the privilege or immunity accorded by the 1961 Act.

A HEARING IN THE JUDGE'S HOME

Sometimes, because of the urgency of an issue such as where one party wants to apply *ex parte* to a judge of the High Court or Circuit Court for a temporary injunction against another party, it becomes necessary for a judge to hold the court in his or her own home. These situations are not uncommon but they can give rise to difficulty for a number of reasons.

The party making the application may not readily cooperate with inquiring reporters, and the judge in whose home the court is to be held may not be too anxious to allow reporters inside.

In approaching this problem, it must be stated that in the generality of cases judges are accommodating in this regard once the journalist acts reasonably. The occasion where the judge refuses access would be the exception.

Except in certain limited cases, justice 'shall' be administered in public, the Constitution states. The fact that the court is held in the judge's home is merely for the convenience of the judge. If the registrar attached to the particular judge is known to the reporter, that person should be contacted as a matter of priority, to arrange attendance at the hearing. If the registrar's identity is not known or cannot be ascertained at short notice, the reporter's only recourse will be to go to the judge's home and seek admission directly.

WHEN IS A PRIVATE COURT HEARING NOT PRIVATE?

Apart from the occasions when the presiding judge allows the media to remain in court to report proceedings while excluding the public and persons with no interest in the particular case, situations can arise where media representatives find themselves in the invidious position of being allowed to stay and report extremely sensitive and delicate matters but only on terms laid down by the judge. One of the most important and controversial cases ever to go before the High Court came within this category. It involved an application under the Adoption Act which went on appeal to the Supreme Court and eventually led to a constitutional referendum.

Similar restrictions apply to judgments in important family law cases such as where the grounds for obtaining an order for the nullity of a marriage are broadened as a result of a particular case. While the identity of the parties is preserved, publication is permitted, as a matter of practice, because of the public importance of the result. Limited reporting of family law cases under the control of the Courts Service has been commenced on a pilot basis in the Circuit Family Court in Dublin.

REPORTS OF JUDICIAL PROCEEDINGS

Before the hearing begins the question often arises whether reporters are free to extract information from files lodged in the central offices of the courts? These files contain copies of the pleadings, such as the Civil Bill and the Defence, the High Court Summons, the Statement of Claim, the Notice for Particulars, the Reply to the Notice, and the Defence, and possibly Affidavits. At District Court level, the Civil Process may be required in advance in civil cases or the summons or charge sheet.

More often than not, the court clerk or Garda sergeant will make the documents available for perusal in the District Court on request, provided the request is reasonably made at a time which does not interfere with the running of the case or disrupt the business at hand; the registrars of the higher courts will also do so; but sometimes a journalist will 'get wind' of perhaps a controversial court case in advance of the date fixed for the hearing and may need to see the documents already on file. The question arises whether the journalist is entitled to see them and to extract information from them.

Similarly, when a case has concluded, reporters are often left in a very difficult position, particularly at country venues when the court rises and the court staff depart, taking the court documents with them. A reporter may be left with no option but to seek the co-operation of a garda to get some piece of information such as details from a summons, for example. This should not be the situation. Basic details such as names, addresses and other information from the documents must be reported accurately and it is incumbent on court staff, no matter how busy they may be, to facilitate reporters in this regard.

It may be going too far to argue that the files in any of the central offices of the courts are open for public inspection and that reporters have a right, within reason, to inspect them and extract information from them. The official view is that only the parties concerned with the particular case, including their legal advisers, may have access to the files. The question has never been tested in court, although one High Court judge some years ago directed an inquiry to be held after extracts from documents on file appeared in a Dublin newspaper prior to a particular hearing.

If the file contains only details of the plaintiff's claim and this is published in advance of the hearing, the report hardly does justice to the defendant named in the suit. This is a question which the newly established Courts Service should address as a matter of priority because it has long been a thorny issue with those charged with the responsibility of reporting the courts throughout the entire country.

THE REPORT

When reporting a court case, the sworn evidence of the witnesses should be relied on rather than speeches of solicitor or counsel. All too frequently the opening speech is reported, particularly where the harassed reporter is working to an early deadline. The reporter hurries away to telephone, fax or transmit by computer the copy to the office without waiting to hear any evidence. If and when the reporter returns to the courtroom later, much of the evidence will have been given and the reporter is left to pick up the pieces and compile a report for later publication from whatever is left of the day's hearing. It may even be that the case was settled while the court was unattended by reporters. Fairness and accuracy have been sacrificed in the interests of expediency.

Care should be taken to report the proceedings accurately and as fully as possible. The summing-up of the judge in criminal trials should also be reported. To be fair and accurate the report need not be *verbatim*. It may be abridged or condensed but it should not be lop-sided with undue emphasis on one side. Since the plaintiff is first in to bat in a civil case and the prosecution is first in in a criminal case, it is too easy to fall into the trap of over-emphasising one side of the argument to the exclusion of the respondent or defendant. If a one-sided view of the case is published, this *could, prima facie,* constitute malice and leave the publisher without the defence of privilege.

THE 'PICK-UP'

One of the greatest pit-falls for publishers and broadcasters is the court report that has been picked-up by one reporter from another. This situation has not been helped by the number of courts that individual reporters may be responsible for covering. Cut-backs have resulted in fewer reporters being assigned on a regular basis to individual courts, particularly in urban areas, with the consequence that the reporter is directed or expected to pick-up a report from one or more courts.

At the best of times, publishing can be a risky business, but the news editor who so directs a reporter – either a member of the staff or a free-lance – is inviting trouble. It is far better for a particular court case to go unreported than for a story to be picked-up latent with error. There have been several instances of this over the years

NAMES AND ADDRESSES

As with so many other facets of reporting, extreme care should be taken to ensure that the names and addresses of the respective parties to an action are transcribed accurately, in addition to particulars of the claim and defence (in civil proceedings) and of the charge in the indictment (in criminal prosecutions). The only short-cut permissible is abbreviating details of the charge or the attached particulars of the charge. With regard to names and addresses, giving the number of the house as stated in the official documents may often lead to problems. The party may have left the house and the new occupier may take exception to owning a property now in the full glare of publicity. Equally, a policy of not giving the number of the house can be troublesome where, for instance, there might be two or even more persons with the same name on the same road in towns or large urban areas. Provincial newspapers are particularly vulnerable because of the proliferation of similar Christian and surnames in areas of the country, frequently in the same village.

However, once the name and address given in the court document are transcribed and published accurately as they appear, privilege should offer protection. In the interests of complete accuracy and in fairness to the aggrieved party, the newspaper should, and usually does, publish a correction or clarification as soon as possible, even though the error is not fundamentally of its making.

THIRD PARTIES

It may happen that reference is made in the course of a court hearing to something that is allegedly said by a person who is not in court or, indeed, that blame may be levied on such a third party, who does not have the opportunity to rebut the statement in court.

While the newspaper is protected by privilege if it reports such statements accurately in an open court hearing, the editor is placed somewhat in a dilemma when the third party seeks redress by the publication of a disclaimer or apology. The newspaper is not a court of law to test the accuracy of the original statement or of the rebutting evidence of the third party. In such circumstances, the editor or, preferably, the newspaper's solicitors should advise the complainant to make a statement in open court, which then can be reported with the protection of privilege.

HEADINGS

The sub-editor who writes the headings on court reports carries a heavy responsibility. With a tendency to sensationalize or to oversimplify, it is relatively easy to fall into the trap of completely misrepresenting the story-line in court copy. The financial consequences to the publisher can be just as grave as in the ordinary case of the publication of a libel.

4

Restrictions on reporting of court cases

Some restrictions have already been referred to but what follows is an attempt to provide a reference to most of the restrictions that are in place at present.

Except in exceptional circumstances, the media has a constitutional right under Article 34 (1) of access to court sittings. The most recent authority for this statement is contained in the Supreme Court judgment in *Irish Times Ltd & Ors v. Judge Anthony Murphy* (2 April 1998). The court found the constitutional requirement that justice should be administered in public should be adhered to, save in exceptional circumstances, and that impeding media access to courts was equivalent to limiting public access.

Despite this freedom, there are numerous restrictions in place. While various pieces of legislation refer to cases being held 'otherwise than in public,' '*in camera,*' or 'in chambers,' the effect in all such cases is to restrict reporting. Where the word 'may' is used, the judge has a discretion; whether to hold the case in public or in private; where the word 'shall' is used, the judge has no such discretion, it is a mandatory restriction.

1 Under the District Court Rules members of the public *may* be excluded: (a) in criminal proceedings for an offence which in the opinion of the court is of an indecent or obscene nature (s. 20 of the Criminal Justice Act, 1951) and (b) where a preliminary hearing for an indictable offence exists to put the accused on trial before a jury (s. 16 of the Criminal Procedure Act, 1967).

However, the legislation states that bona fide members of the Press cannot be excluded from the hearings. Nevertheless, there is still a restriction on reporting under the 1967 Act.

Section 17 of the Act states (my italics) that 'No person shall publish or cause to publish any information as to any particular *preliminary examination* other than a statement of the fact that such examination in relation to a *named* person on a *specified charge* has been held and of the decision thereon.'

The section goes on to provide that the restriction shall not apply to the publication of such information as the judge permits to be published *at the request of the accused.*

2 The Children's Act, 1908 provides for the hearing of charges involving children (under 15) and young persons (15 to 17 years) in Juvenile Courts. Only officers of the court and the parties (including witnesses) together with their legal representatives shall attend unless the court rules otherwise in specific cases. The Act provides that bona fide members of a newspaper or news agency *shall not be excluded.*

The Act does not impose a restriction on the reporting of names. However, there is a convention that the identity of the accused juveniles should not be published.

3 Affiliation proceedings: Section 3 (5) of the Illegitimate Children (Affiliation Orders) Act, 1930 as inserted by s. 28 of the Family Law (Maintenance of Spouses and Children) Act 1976, provides that: 'proceedings under this Act shall be conducted otherwise than in public' while s. 3 (6), also inserted by the 1976 Act, provides that 'it shall not be lawful to permit or publish or cause to be printed or published any material relating to proceedings under this Act which would tend to identify the parties to the proceedings.'

4 Section 45 of the Courts (Supplemental Provisions) Act, 1961 provides that justice *may* be administered otherwise than in public in the following cases:

(a) Applications of an urgent nature for relief by way of habeas corpus, bail, prohibition or injunction (e.g. 'Anton Pilar' injunctions to seize counterfeit goods, such as videos or computer software).
(b) Matrimonial causes or matters.
(c) Lunacy and minor matters.
(d) Proceedings involving the disclosure of a secret manufacturing process.

On 28 March 2000, a High Court judge hearing an application for an injunction pending the trial of the substantive action brought on behalf of two minors by their mother against the board of management of a school which had expelled one and suspended the other for alleged use by them of illicit substances, rejected their application to have reporting restrictions imposed so that their identities would not be revealed. In a written judgment he ruled that where the court was asked to impose limitations on reporting in a particular case, in the absence of clear jurisdiction, the court was bound by the constitutional provision that justice shall be administered in public except in special cases as may be prescribed by law (see *Wright v. Board of Management of Gorey Community School,* O'Sullivan J., High Court, 2000).

5 Company law: The High Court has exercised its discretion to hold *in camera* certain applications brought under the Companies Act, 1963.

Section 205 of the 1963 Act provides that a member of a company may apply to the High Court for relief where the powers of the directors of a company are being exercised or its affairs conducted in a manner oppressive to him or any of the members.

Sub-section 7 of section 205 (7) of the Act provides that: 'If, in the opinion of the court, the hearing of proceedings under this section would involve the disclosure of information the publication of which would be seriously prejudicial to the legitimate interests of the company, the court may order that the hearing or any part of it shall be held *in camera*.'

In a case entitled *In re R. Limited* the Supreme Court in 1989 ruled against the company and one of its directors who applied to have the hearing under section 205 held in private. Finding against them the court held that one of the requirements essential to the administration of justice was that court proceedings be in public unless that requirement, by itself, operated to deny justice in the particular case and this principle was enshrined in Article 34 (1) of the Constitution.

The court also ruled that an *in camera* order duly made under section 205 (7) may in the appropriate case include an order prohibiting the publication of the contents of originating documents and affidavits.

6 Adoption Acts: Provision to hold *in camera* the hearing of questions of law referred to the High Court by the Adoption Board to protect the identity of the parties.

7 Income Tax Appeals: Section 30 of the Finance Act, 1949 provides for the hearing *in camera* of appeals in income tax assessments. Appeals are heard by a Circuit Court judge sitting *in camera* but cases stated are heard by the High Court in open court.

8 Official Secrets: Section 12 of the Official Secrets Act, 1963 provides that if in the course of certain proceedings as set out in the Act application is made by the prosecution, on the ground that the publication of any evidence or statement to be given or made during any part of the hearing would be prejudicial to the safety or preservation of the State, that part of the hearing should be held *in camera,* the court *shall* make an order to that effect but the verdict and sentence (if any) *shall* be announced in public.

9 Censorship: Section 14 of the Censorship of Publication Act, 1929 contains a provision for the restricted reporting of judicial proceedings, including divorce, nullity of marriage and judicial separation. Specifically, it restricts the publication of 'indecent matter the publication of which would be calculated to injure public morals'.

10 Rape cases: the Criminal Law (Rape) Act, 1981 imposes a strict ban on reporting. Section 7 provides that after a person is charged with a rape offence no matter likely to lead members of the public to identify a woman as the complainant in relation to that charge shall be published in a written publication available to the public or be broadcast except as authorised by a direction given in pursuance of this section. This restriction may be relaxed or removed by the judge in certain circumstances (s. 7).

Section 8 provides that *after* a person is charged with a rape offence, no matter likely to lead members of the public to identify him as the person against whom the charge is made shall be published except (a) as authorised by a direction given by the court or (b) *after* he has been convicted of the offence. This restriction may be lifted by direction from the judge in similar circumstances as in the case of a complainant (s. 7).

While there is no time limit on the duration of the restriction in the case of a complainant, the restriction in the case of a person charged ceases after he has been convicted. However, a trial judge has discretion to continue the restriction indefinitely in certain circumstances, e.g. if the disclosure of his identity is likely to lead to the identity of the complainant being revealed.

11 Sexual offences: Criminal Law (Rape) (Amendment) Act, 1990: Sections 7 and 8 of the Criminal Law (Rape) Act, 1981 were amended by Sections 14 and 17 of the 1990 Act. The reporting ban as it applies in rape cases applies to sexual assault offence hearings but only to protect the identity of the victim, not the accused. However, the trial judge may order that the accused should not be identified.

12 Reporting of *all* court cases – civil and criminal: Section 18 (1) of the Defamation Act, 1961 states: 'A *fair* and *accurate* report published in any newspaper or broadcast by means of wireless telegraphy as part of any programme or service provided by means of a broadcasting station within the State or in Northern Ireland of proceedings publicly heard before any court established by law and exercising judicial authority within the State or in Northern Ireland shall, if published or broadcast contemporaneously with such proceedings, be privileged.'

13 Section 18 (2) of the Defamation Act, 1961 provides that nothing in subsection 1 of s. 18 (see No. 11 above) shall authorise the publication or broadcasting of any blasphemous or obscene matter.

14 Criminal trials: During the course of a criminal trial in the Circuit Court or the Central Criminal Court, there may be legal argument between counsel and the Judge in the absence of the jury. Even though reporters may be present on these occasions, nothing that is said during the absence of the jury can be reported.

Situations can often arise during the course of a criminal trial where some piece of evidence, such as, for example, whether a statement made to the gardaí by the defendant was admissible (i.e. to be allowed into evidence). There may even be evidence on these occasions with witnesses giving evidence and being cross-examined. These are often referred to and reported as 'a trial within a trial'. The entire prosecution case may depend on whether the piece of evidence under consideration or the defendant's statement in this example is allowed into evidence. The defence may challenge the statement as not having been voluntarily made or having been made by the defendant in breach of a constitutional right.

If a reporter were to report what went on in the absence of the jury, the case could be made that such publication or broadcast prejudiced the defendant's right to a fair trial. The likely outcome would be that the jury would be discharged, the trial adjourned to some future date and the radio station summoned to appear before the trial judge to answer why it should not be held guilty of contempt.

Equally, the defendant's previous convictions or criminal character are often known before the trial itself. Under no circumstances may these be referred to in a publication or broadcast prior to conviction. Judges have very wide powers in this area and the reality is that the editor or radio executive in charge of news and the reporter concerned would be heavily fined in terms of having to pay a large sum of money to the court for the contempt in addition to having to offer a sincere apology for the breach.

15 Comment after conviction: This is a grey area, especially in the absence of legislation in this area. It could arise where the radio station or newspaper decides to publish a background item or comment piece on a person following conviction but before sentence was passed. This may include a wide trawl or history of his involvement in crime and include material that was not put before the court. Strictly speaking, the matter is still *sub judice*. While the person's lawyers will do what they can to get the lightest penalty possible for their client, they could argue that the wide publicity given to the background item could prejudice the defendant's right to a fair trial in that, for example, the published material created bias in the mind of the Judge.

In a recent decision the Supreme Court ruled that it could be contempt to publish such an article *after* conviction but *before* sentencing and that this could be the case despite the guarantee of freedom of expression in Article 40 of the Constitution.

To take matters a step further, it is conceivable that a court would view this restriction as remaining in place until after a convicted person's appeal has been disposed of or, if he/she does not actually appeal, until after the time in which an appeal may be lodged has expired. It must be remembered that no two cases are alike and just because a publisher 'gets away' with publication of such details in one case, it does not mean that a problem will not arise in another case.

16 Criminal libel: Section 8 of the Defamation Act, 1961 provides, in part, that no criminal prosecution shall be commenced against any proprietor, publisher, editor or any person responsible for the publication of a newspaper for any libel it publishes without an order of a judge of the High Court sitting *in camera* being first obtained.

17 Incest prosecutions: The Criminal Law (Incest Proceedings) (No. 2) Act, 1995 repealed section 5 of the Punishment of Incest Act, 1908. The latter legislation provided that all proceedings under that Act were to be conducted *in camera*. However, the 1995 Act introduced a more liberal reporting regime, similar to that applying in rape trials.

18 Criminal assets: Section 10 of the Criminal Assets Bureau Act, 1996 preserves the anonymity of a bureau officer or an officer of the Minister for Social Welfare or any member of the staff of the Bureau. They cannot be identified to any person other than to a judge hearing a case brought under the Act in which they are witnesses. The Act also provides that such witnesses may give their evidence in the hearing but not in the sight of any person. Section 11 of the Act provides that a person who publishes the identity of such persons or even the address of family members of the witnesses shall be guilty of an offence and be liable on summary conviction to a maximum fine of £1500 or to 12 months' imprisonment or both, or on conviction on indictment to a maximum fine of £50,000 or three years in prison or both.

19 Proceeds of crime: Proceedings brought under the Proceeds of Crime Act, 1996 in which an interim order was sought must be heard otherwise than in public. The Act also provides that any other proceedings brought under the Act may, if the respondent or any other party to the proceedings (other than the applicant) so requests and the court considers it proper, be heard otherwise than in public.

5

Contempt of court

The essence of contempt of court is action or inaction amounting to interference with or obstruction to, or having a tendency to interfere with or to obstruct, the due administration of justice.

That definition from an old English case is cited by one of the main standard textbooks on criminal law, *Archbold.* An even shorter definition would be 'conduct offensive to a court of law or prejudicial to the course of justice'.

Mr Justice Seamus Henchy, former Supreme Court judge and former chairman of the Independent Radio and Television Commission, said that contempt of court, whether civil or criminal, whether committed in the face of the court or out of court, whether committed in relation to imminent, to pending, or to past proceedings, is a remedy primarily, not at upholding the dignity of a court or a judge, but at enabling the administration of justice to operate without due obstruction or interference.

More recently, the Chief Justice, Mr Justice Ronan Keane, said contempt occurs when a person publishes something calculated to interfere with the course of justice. It was not necessary that it resulted in such interference.

Civil contempt is a method of enforcing court orders. It also deals with disobedience of orders by courts. However, journalists are more concerned with *criminal contempt,* which is a crime. This form of contempt represents the law's proscription of conduct as a crime deemed to be incompatible with the proper administration of justice. It very much affects journalists. It can be tried by a judge summarily of his own motion or it can arise as a result of an application to a judge by one of or both of the parties to a civil action or a criminal prosecution.

The applicant must discharge the criminal burden of proof, i.e. beyond a reasonable doubt, that a publication or a broadcast had been a contempt of court. When the court is satisfied that contempt had been proved, the judge has wide discretion in the form of penalty he can impose on the transgressor. It can be imprisonment, fine, security for good behaviour or an injunction to restrain repetition of the act found to constitute contempt.

When a case is pending which may ultimately be tried before a court, the common law rule is that nothing can be published which might interfere with the course of justice, even though the publication was due to a genuine mistake on the part of the reporter and was published in good faith with no intention to interfere with the course of justice. In very serious forms of criminal contempt the court may seek to establish the *mens rea*, i.e. the guilty mind or intention by the journalist and/or the publisher to commit the crime.

The possibility of contempt of court proceedings lurks in every court. A simple bail application by an accused can, conceivably, lead to contempt proceedings if material is published concerning the accused which might interfere with the accuser's right to a fair trial. If, in the course of the bail application, a Garda witness testifies to the fact that he saw the accused rob a bank or discharge a firearm at pursuing members of the Force, publication of this evidence, even innocently, could prejudice the accuser's subsequent trial before a jury. A court trying the contempt issue would adjudicate on the basis that the jurors might have read the newspaper report or heard the broadcast bulletin and so would have a preconceived idea about the guilt of the accused. When such breaches occur the accuser's trial is normally adjourned for a long period to remedy, by the passage of time, whatever damage might have been caused.

A newspaper is also guilty of contempt of court if it refers to a previous conviction of the accused prior to the court or the jury having an opportunity to decide his guilt or innocence based on the evidence before them (see chapter 4).

A 'prelim' report published about an accused in advance of the trial is also technically in contempt of court. There have been several instances of this, where criminal trials were aborted so that the editor and, possibly, the publisher could be called to task before the court.

Mistake or inadvertence does not excuse this breach, any more than it does in the case of defamation. The offence is committed if the publication is deemed likely to interfere with the fair trial that an accused is constitutionally entitled to. An Irish case decided that the power to attach for contempt may be exercised against a corporate body, i.e. the company which owned and/or published the newspaper concerned in the contempt issue.

A High Court judge presiding over a murder trial in the Central Criminal Court, banned the publication of comment on or photographs of the woman accused before the court during her trial. The basis of the ban was the accused's right to a fair trial, which according to the judge, far out-weighed the media's right to comment on her appearance or demeanour (*Irish Times*, 10 February 2000).

Various pieces of legislation expressly give courts and tribunals powers to deal with contempt issues. In chapter 4, reference was made to section 17 (1) of the Criminal Procedure Act, 1967 to illustrate the legislative prohibition on the publication of preliminary examinations in the District Court. Sub-section (2) of the same section goes on to state:

> If it appears to a justice of the District Court, on the application of the Attorney General, that any person has contravened sub-section (1), he may certify to that effect under his hand to the High Court and the court may thereupon inquire into the alleged offence and after hearing any witnesses who may be produced against or on behalf of that person, and after hearing any statement that may be offered in defence, publish or take steps for the punishment of that person in the like manner as if he had been found guilty of contempt of court.

Just how thin the line is between what is permissible and what is not when a judge makes an order prohibiting publication of certain matter can be gauged from a recent experience of a newspaper editor. He received copy from a freelance journalist who omitted to inform him of a direction by the trial judge at a sexual assault or sexual abuse trial in the Dublin Circuit Court that only the name of the province where the parties resided could be published; the name of the city in which the events giving rise to the charges could not. Being unaware of the judge's order, the editor, in order to localise the story, identified the city but within hours of his newspaper appearing on the street he was summoned to appear before the court the following morning where he was fined £6,000 for contempt of the judge's order, despite strong argument by his counsel that the breach was total inadvertence by the newspaper.

PHOTOGRAPHERS AND CONTEMPT

Photo-journalists and cameramen are frequently assigned to photograph accused persons and witnesses as they enter and emerge from court buildings before, during and after trials. Does the publication of such photographs amount to contempt, particularly if they appear during the currency of the trial? The publication of a photograph or film of an accused can amount to contempt where visual identification of the accused must either be, or be reasonably likely to be in issue at the trial. The rule is that publication of a photograph at a time when identity is likely to come into issue amounts to contempt. One reason for this is that the publication may prejudice the accused's right to a fair trial by fostering an inaccurate identification.

An example of this is where a person is brought before a District Court for the purpose of being formally charged, say with murder, and his arrival or departure from the court is recorded and subsequently broadcast on television. That same footage may be used several times after numerous remand appearances by the accused. When the trial eventually begins, the issue of identification becomes a crucial factor in the trial. Jurors may have seen the previously published television footage of the accused and may be influenced by it to the accused's detriment. Equally, the publication could prejudice the prosecution by diminishing the value of an identification witness.

SCANDALIZING THE COURT

A daily newspaper published a statement in good faith that it had received from an organization. They accepted the *bona fides* of the source of the statement and duly published it. The joint authors of the particular statement criticized the Special Criminal Court to such an extent that the Supreme Court, on appeal by the defendants from the High Court, ruled that they had scandalized the court and remitted the case to the High Court to allow the joint authors to be dealt with. The situation that the newspaper found itself in – although its *bona fides* was accepted by the court was little different from the other Dublin newspaper which published a letter from a reader in good faith but ended up in the dock for contempt. Both situations show that great care must be exercised where the letter or statement purports to reflect on the character, capacity or motives of an identified or identifiable person or, as we have seen, of a court.

The essence of this form of contempt, which is rare, is that the statement tends to lower the authority of the court and brings it into odium or derision.

COMMENT ON COURT PROCEEDINGS

Although there is a right to publish a fair and accurate report contemporaneously with the court proceedings, no comment on them should be published while the proceedings are still before the court. Comment is permissible only when the case is finally concluded and the decision is announced in a civil action or, in a criminal prosecution, by the conviction or acquittal of the defendant. The question might be asked whether it is possible to offer comment or to publish a follow-up story in relation to a decided civil action if the decision is going to be appealed. Under the rules governing the operation of the courts, a given period is allowed in which to lodge a notice of appeal – for example, a party to a High Court action is allowed 21 days. There should be no expression of opinion, no colouring of a report of facts, whether by emphasis or by omission, during the currency of a court hearing; newspapers, however, usually hold themselves free to comment on a case once it is concluded, even where the appeal notice has been lodged in the higher court. Each case must be viewed on its own circumstances. In one case involving an Irish magazine, where extended coverage had been given to a pending case, the judge hearing the contempt proceedings decided not to hold the publisher in contempt for the reason that such prior publicity could not be prejudicial since the case about which comment had been made was to be tried by a judge. A different view would probably have been taken were it to have come before a jury. Nonetheless, if an editor knows as a fact that proceedings are imminent or that an appeal is pending before any court, comment should be withheld until the case is finally determined. To act otherwise is to invite trouble.

The most recent judicial pronouncement on post-conviction comment came in a Supreme Court judgment in December 1999 in which the court lamented the absence of legislation on contempt in this country. The court ruled that a newspaper article about a criminal which was published after his conviction but before he was sentenced, could be a contempt of court. Whether the article did constitute contempt would have to be determined by the High Court, taking into account all the circumstances, some of which had not been established at the time of the Supreme Court appeal hearing. Specifically, the five judges replied in the affirmative to the following two questions posed: (1) Can it be a contempt of court to publish an article in the terms complained of after a criminal trial has passed from the seisin (control) of the jury and where the remainder of the hearing will take place before a judge sitting alone, and (2) Given the constitutional right to freedom of expression of the Press, could the publication of the article complained of ever constitute a contempt of court before a judge sitting alone? Coincidentally, the court found there was an absence of *men rea* or guilty intent on the part of both the editor and the author of the article concerned.

The content of the article, of course, is fundamentally important and the Supreme Court was not stating that every article written or broadcast post-conviction and prior to sentencing, would amount to contempt. The article in question contained allegations derived from garda sources and not adduced in evidence before the trial judge.

Since then, Carney J, sitting in the Central Criminal Court, commented on the Supreme Court judgment. He said his interpretation of the judgment was that there had been a shift of emphasis towards the dangers of prejudicial coverage between conviction and sentence, and even before the disposal of final appeal. The judgment, he said, was less concerned with the effects of newspaper coverage on judges than on the perception of an accused that he was getting the fair administration of justice. Tabloid newspapers might have taken the view that they were free of restraint from the moment of conviction but, he advised, restraint might apply even between sentence and the disposal of final appeal. He was ruling on a contempt motion relating to the content of a headline used in a tabloid newspaper during the course of a trial (*Irish Times*, 22 January 2000).

JURY DISAGREEMENT

Are journalists free to comment after a criminal trial has concluded with the jury disagreeing as to the guilt of the accused? There is legal authority for the proposition that the restraints appropriate to a pending trial continue to apply to this situation regarding contempt.

THE 'SUB JUDICE' RULE

This form of contempt has been defined as follows: Contempt will be established if a publication has a tendency to interfere with the due administration of justice in the particular proceedings. This tendency is to be determined objectively by reference to the nature of the publication. It is not relevant for this purpose to determine what the actual effect of the publication upon the proceedings has been, or what it probably will be. If the publication is of a character which might have an effect upon the proceedings, it will have the necessary tendency, unless the possibility of interference is so remote or theoretical that the *de minimis* principle (i.e. the interference is so small that it can be eliminated) should be applied.

The *sub judice* rule has been a cause of much controversy over the years and a particular thorn in the side of news editors and investigative journalists.

As previously explained, a civil action is begun by issuing a summons or writ; a criminal prosecution by the issuing of a warrant or summons. Once this has been done, the proceedings are *sub judice*, and no comment is permitted. In other words, once a question – civil or criminal – has passed into the domain of the courts for judicial determination, any conduct calculated to interfere with the functions of the court could bring wrath, in the form of proceedings for criminal contempt, down on the heads of the violators. For a breach to have occurred, it would be necessary for the originating writ or summons to have been issued.

An inquiring journalist is often met with a statement that a matter is *sub-judice* because the issue in controversy has been handed to a solicitor or simply because a solicitor's letter has been sent on behalf of one party to another party in a particular dispute. In such circumstances, that issue would not be *sub judice* because, according to the definition given at the outset, the rule only refers to 'in the proceedings.' If no proceedings have been commenced with the issuing and service of an originating summons or other document, they cannot be *sub judice*.

The rule would very much apply to situations where a suspect is brought before a District Court and charged with a criminal offence. Once the person is charged, nothing but the facts adduced in open court may be published. These include evidence of arrest, the accused's name and address, details of the charge and the remand.

THE CONSTITUTIONAL GUARANTEE OF FREEDOM OF EXPRESSION

The Constitution guarantees the right of citizens to express freely their convictions and opinions but as with most rights this guarantee is not limitless. The fundamental rights portion of the Bunreacht, while expressing the right, states:

> The education of public opinion being, however, a matter of such grave import to the common good, the State shall endeavour to ensure that organs of public opinion, such as the radio, the press, the cinema, while preserving their rightful liberty of expression, including criticism of Government policy, shall not be used to undermine public order or morality or the authority of the State ...

Earlier, we have endeavoured to state the law as it is and has been applied by the Irish courts when the question of contempt arises in relation to comment on pending court proceedings and the *sub judice* rule. The parameters of the law are never fixed, and each new case that comes before the courts is capable of opening up new horizons and further loosening of the fetters that bind media comment. When editors are trying to make an on-the-spot decision as to whether they should publish or not, they may get some guidance from the following comments by a judge of the High Court, which are as appropriate today as they were when first delivered in 1987:

> I do not see why a judgment cannot be criticised provided it is not done in a matter calculated to bring the Court or the judge into contempt. If that element is not present, there is no reason why judgments should not be criticised. Nor does the criticism have to be confined to scholarly articles in legal journals. The mass media are entitled to have their say as well. The public takes a great interest in court cases and it is only natural that discussion should concentrate on the result of cases. So criticism which does not subvert justice should be allowed ...

6

Privacy

Everybody values their privacy and very often go to extreme lengths to protect it. But what is the legal position regarding privacy – the right to be left alone, or freedom from human interference by any means, including surveillance and the prying journalist?

Apart from the constitutional right to marital privacy read into the Constitution by the Supreme Court in 1972 and other such rights implied by the court, no tort or civil wrong for breach of privacy has been created. The Law Reform Commission pointed out in 1998 that Irish positive law had failed to deliver a comprehensive and effective means of protection for privacy. However, there is considerable protection for isolated aspects of privacy available to the public, some of which are set out below.

TRESPASS

The civil wrong of trespass gives generous protection of privacy interests: any wrongful entry onto property is actionable without the plaintiff having to prove that damage was caused. There is similar protection for trespass to a person's goods as well as trespass to the person.

NUISANCE

Nuisance is another actionable wrong and provides a remedy under which a person may sue in order to protect his privacy. An action taken in an English High Court some years ago provides some assistance in considering the extent, at least, to which photographers are permitted to photograph a person's private property.

In the particular case, an aerial photograph was shot of the plaintiff's residence, and the plaintiff, a lord of the realm, sued, but the court decided that the defendant was not liable in trespass because the plane had not flown unreasonably low over the property.

The judge, in delivering his decision, said he did not wish the judgment to be understood as deciding that in no circumstances could a successful action be brought against an aerial photographer to restrain his activities. He said:

> The present action is not founded in nuisance for no court would regard the taking of a single photograph as an actionable nuisance. But if the circumstances were such that a plaintiff was subjected to the harassment of constant surveillance of his home from the air, accompanied by the photographing of his every activity, I am far from saying that the court would not regard such a monstrous invasion of his privacy as an actionable nuisance for which they would give relief.

HARASSMENT – A CRIMINAL SANCTION

Since the enactment in this country of the Non-Fatal Offences against the Person Act, 1997 there is a new statutory offence of harassment which, conceivably, could be used by a member of the public to bring a complaint to the Gardaí in order to deter a pestering journalist.

Section 10 (1) of the 1997 Act states that any person who, without lawful authority or reasonable excuse, by any means including by use of the telephone, harasses another by persistently following, watching, pestering, besetting or communicating with him or her, shall be guilty of an offence. The words 'without lawful authority or reasonable excuse' would, no doubt, be very important to an inquiring journalist who would seek to justify his or her actions in a defence to a charge under this section. The section also defines what is meant by harass. According to subsection (2) a person harasses another where (a) he or she, by his or her acts, intentionally or recklessly, seriously interferes with the other's peace and privacy or causes alarm, distress or harm to the other, and (b) his or her acts are such that a reasonable person would realise that the acts would seriously interfere with the other's peace and privacy or cause alarm, distress or harm to the other.

The judge is empowered to order that a person found guilty of a charge under section 10 shall not communicate with the other person or shall not approach within a specified distance of the other person's place of residence or employment. A person found guilty under the section is liable on summary conviction in the District Court to a fine not exceeding £1,500 or to a maximum of twelve months' imprisonment or both or, on conviction on indictment, to a fine or to imprisonment for a term not exceeding seven years or to both (see also p. 34).

BREACH OF CONFIDENCE

Protection is also given by the law where there has been a breach of confidence by the disclosure of information which was confidentially obtained. Where contract is not relied upon, the plaintiff must establish three elements in his claim: firstly, the information must have 'the necessary quality about it', that is, it must not be something which is public property and public knowledge; secondly, the information must have been imparted in circumstances importing an obligation of confidence, and thirdly, there must be an unauthorized use of the information to the detriment of the party communicating it.

At the outset of this topic, mention was made of the Supreme Court appeal which gave life to the constitutional right to marital privacy. In that same case, one of the Supreme Court judges in the course of his judgment stated:

Whilst the 'personal rights' [under the Constitution] are not described specifically, it is scarcely to be doubted in our society that the right to privacy is universally recognised and accepted with possibly the rarest of exceptions.

In this country, there is, as yet, no Press Council to which such complaints could be made and redress sought. However, there is a Broadcasting Complaints Commission which was established under the Broadcasting Authority (Amendment) Act, 1976, which is empowered by section 18 to investigate and decide a range of complaints.

The Independent Radio and Television Act, 1988 provided for the establishment of the Independent Radio and Television Commission. There is strict monitoring of the output by stations under its remit. All commercial stations are notified of breaches of the advertising and sponsorship codes.

DATA PROTECTION

In July 1988 the Data Protection Act came into force. It gives protection in the context of the privacy of individuals with regard to the automated processing of personal data. This would be mainly personal data retained on computers and word processors. The Act also regulates the collection, processing, use and disclosure of certain information relating to individuals. Personal data is information recorded on a computer about living, identifiable individuals.

Under the Act a data controller should in respect of personal data kept by him comply with the following: the data or the information constituting the data should be processed fairly, be accurate and kept up to date, be kept for one or more specified and lawful purposes and should not be used or disclosed in any manner incompatible with purpose or those purposes. There is also a provision that that personal data must be kept for no longer than is necessary for the specified purposes. In addition, it is specifically provided that appropriate security measures must be taken against unauthorised access to, alteration, disclosure or destruction of the data and against their accidental loss or corruption.

Journalists are not given any privilege under the Act in relation to their files.

FREEDOM OF INFORMATION

The Freedom of Information Act, 1997 gives protection against the disclosure of personal or private information. However, that protection can be overridden if the public interest in disclosure outweighs the public interest in secrecy. There is a presumption of openess in the Act and if public officials want to maintain secrecy and refuse access to official records dating back to 21 April 1998 being sought by journalists, they have to justify that refusal.

The preamble to the Act describes the Act as, including 'an Act to enable members of the public to obtain access, to the greatest extent possible consistent with the public interest and the right to privacy, to information in the possession of public bodies'. The words quoted were highlighted by a High Court judge recently in one of the first cases taken in relation to the 1997 Act (see *Minister for Agriculture v. Information Commissioner*, O'Donovan J, 17 December 1999). In the same judgment he said that except in those cases where access to records was specifically prohibited by the Act e.g. an exempt record within the meaning of section 2 (1) of the Act, there was a very heavy onus on a public body, which refused to grant access to records sought from it, to justify that refusal.

PUBLIC'S RIGHT TO KNOW

The public's right to know has been accorded priority status in a number of cases in recent years. In a case which had an important bearing on the

Cooper-Flynn v. RTE & Others libel action result in the High Court, the Supreme Court ruled in *National Irish Bank Ltd and National Irish Bank Financial Services Ltd v. RTE* in March 1998 that there was a clear public interest in the disclosure by the media of allegations of serious misconduct to the public at large. The court weighed the public's right to know about allegations of misconduct by the bank, against the bank's and its customers' rights to confidentiality.

The 'people's right' to know certain information is evident in the Supreme Court decision upholding media publicity with a criminal trial and with the discretion of trial judges in controlling the same in the interests of the administration of justice (see Chapter 4).

THE RIGHT TO BE LEFT ALONE

The former Chief Justice, the late Mr Justice Hamilton, in 1987 preferred to call the right to privacy 'the right to be left alone' and said in the course of his judgment:

> Though not specifically guaranteed by the Constitution, the right of privacy is one of the fundamental personal rights of the citizen which flows from the Christian and democratic nature of the State. It is not an unqualified right. Its exercise may be restricted by the con-stitutional right of others, by the requirements of the common good, and it is subject to the requirements of public order and morality. The action of the executive in 'tapping' the telephones of two journalists without any lawful authority, and in interfering with and intruding upon the privacy of the journalists in question, constituted an attack on their dignity and freedom as individuals and as journalists.

This case led to the enactment of legislation governing telephone interception in the form of the Interception of Postal Packets and Telecommunications Messages (Regulation) Act, 1993.

RECOMMENDATIONS FOR REFORM

In 1998 the Law Reform Commission in its report on privacy recommended the enactment of a new tort (a civil wrong) which would protect the right of privacy against the threat posed by surveillance. This would be directed at 'information privacy' in the main and would embrace the publication of private information no matter how it was obtained. It also recommended the enactment of a related tort of harassment. These recommendations have not been formulated into legislation but as we have shown above, a prosecution can now be brought for the crime of harassment.

It's important to point out that the Commission, under the presidency of Mr Justice Anthony Hederman, stressed that the sort of protection for privacy they envisaged was not a haven for those who might seek to keep information from the public on matters where there was a clear public interest. But they added the caveat: 'Mere newsworthiness is not a reliable proxy for the public interest.'

7

Other topics

JOURNALISTIC PRIVILEGE

The common law does not recognise a privilege known as journalistic privilege. But that is not to say that a court will never have regard to the confidentiality of the communication. In laying down the test for the existence of this privilege, the court said the following conditions must exist: (1) the information must originate in a confidence that the identity of the informant must not be disclosed; (2) the element of confidentiality must be essential to the full and satisfactory maintenance of the relationship between the parties; (3) the relationship must be one which in the opinion of the court should be fostered, and (4) the injury that would result for the relationship by reason of the disclosure of the identity of the informant must be greater than the benefit thus gained for the correct disposal of the proceedings.

There have been few opportunities for the superior courts to consider whether journalistic privilege to refuse to disclose sources of information should be part of the law. The most thorough examination that this issue received was in the Court of Criminal Appeal in 1972 when RTE reporter Kevin O'Kelly refused to identify the voice on a tape recording in a prosecution before the Special Criminal Court. The appeal court in its judgment stated that journalists were not any more constitutionally or legally immune than other citizens from disclosing information received in confidence. 'The fact that a communication was made under terms of expressed confidence or implied confidence does not create a privilege against disclosure. So far as the administration of justice is concerned, the public has a right to everyman's evidence except those persons protected by a constitutional or other established and recognised privilege,' added the three-man court, who commented further: 'the claim of privilege to refuse to answer the question was unsustainable in law although made in good faith.'

Article 10 of the European Convention on Human Rights, discussed above under 'damages' in Chapter 2, adds a further dimension to this issue. It is worth repeating here: 'No court may require a person to disclose, nor is any person guilty of contempt of court for refusing to disclose, the source of information contained in a publication for which he is responsible unless it be established to the satisfaction of the court that disclosure is necessary in the interests of justice or national security or for the prevention of disorder or crime.'

Section 10 of Contempt of Court Act, 1981 was enacted in England to bring their domestic law into line with the right of freedom of expression in Article 10 of the European Convention. In 1997, the High Court in London was faced with injunction proceedings involving Camelot, the then organisers of the National Lottery in Britain. Camelot intended to publish a preliminary financial statement and towards that end they prepared a set of draft end-year accounts. An unknown person sent a copy of the draft accounts to a journalist who wrote an article focussing on the large payouts which the directors of Camelot were said to have awarded themselves whilst the funds allocated to good cases decreased. The article was published in *Marketing Week.* In subsequent proceedings Camelot were granted an injunction directing Centaur Communications, the journalist's employer, to deliver up the draft accounts in their possession. They had sought the order to assist them in identifying the source of the leak while Centaur's concern was to protect the identity of their source. The High Court judge took the view that the public interest in enabling Camelot to discover a disloyal employee who leaked confidential information was greater than the public interest in enabling that person to escape detection.

Centaur appealed the decision to the Court of Appeal. It dismissed the appeal, saying that although the exercise of the court's power to compel the disclosure of a source of information was restricted by section 10 of the Contempt of Court Act, 1981 'unless it be established to the satisfaction of the court that the disclosure is necessary in the interests of justice or national security or for the prevention of disorder or crime', the High Court judge had correctly taken the view that such an order was necessary in the interests of justice.

Decisions of the English superior courts are not binding on the courts in this jurisdiction; they are nonetheless, persuasive. The decision of the English Court of Appeal in this case falls into this category and, perhaps, is an indication of the manner in which this crucial aspect of the law for journalists will develop in this country.

THE OFFICIAL SECRETS ACT, 1963

No journalist in contemporary Irish society would give a minute's thought to the Official Secrets Act, believing that it is designed for the safeguarding of official information within the ambit of State servants with no relevance to the working journalist. But such an assumption would be wrong, despite the recent amendment of the Act by the Freedom of Information Act, 1997.

While the Act *does* provide for the safeguarding of official information, journalists are, or should be, very much concerned with some of its provisions.

'Official information', within the meaning of the Act, means any secret official code word or password, and any sketch, plan, model, article, note, document or information which is secret or confidential or is expressed to be either and which is or has been in the possession, custody or control of a holder of a public office, or to which he has or had access, by virtue of his office, and includes information recorded by film or magnetic tape by any other recording medium.

'Official document' includes a passport, official pass, permit, document of identity, certificate, licence or other similar document, whether or not completed or issued for use, and also includes an endorsement thereon or addition thereto.

'Public office' is stated to mean an office or employment which is wholly remunerated out of the Central Fund or out of moneys provided by the Oireachtas, or an appointment to, or employment under, any commission, committee or tribunal set up by the Government or a Minister for the purpose of an inquiry, but does not include membership of either house of the Oireachtas.

The ambit of the Act and its powers are wide indeed when considered against the above definitions and give wide rein to the Government to institute prosecutions where its law officers consider that there has been a breach. In fact, considering the wide scope of the legislation, it would, perhaps, be surprising that so few prosecutions have been taken over the years, were it not for the fact that Ireland now enjoys a more open form of government with a better flow of information from official sources than was the case a quarter of a century ago.

Part Two of the Act is most relevant for journalists. This deals with the communication of information to the prejudice of the safety or preservation of the State. More specifically, section 9 (1) states: A person shall not, in any manner prejudicial to the safety or preservation of the State –

(a) obtain, record, communicate to any other person or publish, or

(b) have in his possession or under his control any document containing, or other record whatsoever of, information relating to –

   (i) the number, description, armament, equipment, disposition, movement or condition of any of the Defence Forces or of any of the vessels or aircraft belonging to the State,

   (ii) any operations or projected operations of any of the Defence Forces or of the Garda Síochána or of any of the vessels or aircraft belonging to the State,

   (iii) any measures for the defence or fortification of any place on behalf of the State,

   (iv) munitions of war, or

   (v) any other matter whatsoever information as to which would or might be prejudicial to the safety or preservation of the State.

The theft of a racehorse seems a most unlikely cause of a reporter, his editor and their newspaper proprietors being prosecuted under the Official Secrets Act, even when the horse's name is Shergar. But in 1983, in one of two relatively recent prosecutions under the Act, this occurred. The owners of the Dublin newspaper published extracts from a *fógra* or notice circulated to Garda stations throughout the country which contained details of a number of persons Gardaí wanted to question in connection with the disappearance of the horse. Although the District Court acquitted the reporter in question, the editor and the newspaper owners were convicted.

The Official Secrets Act has been amended by section 48 of the Freedom of Information Act, 1997 to provide that a person who reasonable believes that he or she is authorised by the 1997 Act to communicate official information to another person shall be deemed for the purposes of section 4 of the 1963 Act to be duly authorised to communicate that information. Section 4 of the 1963 Act provides that a person shall not communicate any official information to any other person unless he is duly authorised to do so or does so in the course of and in accordance with his duties as the holder of a public office or when it is his duty in the interest of the State to communicate it.

The FOI Act states that in a prosecution for an offence under section 5 or 9 of the 1963 Act it shall be a defence to prove that the act to which the charge of the offence relates is authorised, or is reasonably believed by the person charged to be authorised, by the 1997 Act. When we turn to the 1963 Act we see that section 5 states, among other things, that a party to a contract with a Minister or State authority shall not divulge the contents of the contract expressed in the contract to be confidential while the full contents of section 9 are set out above.

BOOK PUBLISHERS

Although this handbook is designed for journalists, much of what it has to say will be of interest to publishers of books as distinct from newspapers and periodicals. Many journalists, moreover, are the authors of books; in that capacity they may be inclined to think that is what is publishable in a newspaper, for example, is equally publishable in the text of a book. This is not the case for at least one important reason: books do not enjoy the protection of privilege which is given *to contemporaneous* reports of legal proceedings: thus, details of a case as reported, with privilege, in a newspaper cannot automatically be presumed to be publishable in a book which may appear even years later.

8

The National Union of Journalists

The vast majority of journalists working in the media in this country are members of the National Union of Journalists, which introduced a Code of Professional Conduct in 1936. The terms of the code are:

1. A journalist has a duty to maintain the highest professional and ethical standards.

2. A journalist shall at all times defend the principle of the freedom of the Press and other media in relation to the collection of information and the expression of comment and criticism. He/she shall strive to eliminate distortion, news suppression and censorship.

3. A journalist shall strive to ensure that the information he/she disseminates is fair and accurate, avoid the expression of comment and conjecture as established fact and falsification by distortion, selection or misrepresentation.

4. A journalist shall rectify promptly any inaccuracies, ensure that correction and apologies receive due prominence and afford the right of reply to persons criticised when the issue is of sufficient importance.

5. A journalist shall obtain information, photographs and illustrations only by straightforward means. The use of other means can be justified only by overriding considerations of the public interest The journalist is entitled to exercise a personal conscientious objection to the use of such means.

6. Subject to justification by over-riding considerations of the public interest, a journalist shall do nothing which entails intrusion into private grief and distress.

7. A journalist shall protect confidential sources of information.

8. A journalist shall not accept bribes nor shall he/she allow other induce-ments to influence the performance of his/her professional duties.

9. A journalist shall not lend himself/herself to the distortion or suppression of the truth because of advertising or other considerations.

10. A journalist shall only mention a person's race, colour, creed, illegitimacy, marital status or lack of it, gender or sexual orientation if this information is strictly relevant. A journalist shall neither originate nor process material which encourages discrimination on any of the above-mentioned grounds.

11. A journalist shall not take private advantage of information gained in the course of his/her duties, before the information is public knowl-edge.

12. A journalist shall not by way of statement, voice or appearance endorse by advertisement any commercial product or service save for the promotion of his/her own work or of the medium by which he/she is employed.

Punishment by way of fine, suspension or expulsion is provided for in cases of 'conduct detrimental to the interests of the Union or of the profession'.

APPENDIX 1

Defamation Act, 1961

ARRANGEMENT OF SECTIONS

PART I

PRELIMINARY AND GENERAL

PART II

CRIMINAL PROCEEDINGS FOR LIBEL

PART III

CIVIL PROCEEDINGS FOR DEFAMATION

FIRST SCHEDULE

Enactments repealed

SECOND SCHEDULE

Statements having qualified privilege

Number 40 of 1961

DEFAMATION ACT, 1961

AN ACT TO CONSOLIDATE WITH AMENDMENTS CERTAIN
ENACTMENTS RELATING TO THE LAW OF DEFAMATION
[*17th August, 1961.*]

BE IT ENACTED BY THE OIREACHTAS AS FOLLOWS:—

PART I

PRELIMINARY AND GENERAL

Short title   **1.** This Act may be cited as the Defamation Act, 1961.

Interpretation generally, 1941, No. 23

2. In this Act—

"local authority" has the same meaning as in the Local Government Act, 1941;

"newspaper", except in section 27, means any paper containing public news or observations thereon, or consisting wholly or mainly of advertisements, which is printed for sale and is published in the State or in Northern Ireland either periodically or in parts or numbers at intervals not exceeding thirty-six days;

"proprietor" means, as well as the sole proprietor of any newspaper, in the case of a divided proprietorship, the persons who, as partners or otherwise, represent or are responsible for any share or interest in the newspaper as between themselves and the persons in like manner representing or responsible for the other shares or interests therein, and no other person.

Commencement and proceedings affected

3. (1) This Act shall come into operation on the 1st day of January, 1962.

(2) Part III of this Act shall apply for the purposes of any proceedings begun after the commencement of this Act, whenever the

cause of action arose, but shall not affect any proceedings commenced before the commencement of this Act.

4.—The enactments specified in the First Schedule to this Act are hereby repealed.

Repeals

PART II

CRIMINAL PROCEEDINGS FOR LIBEL

5. (1) On every trial of an indictment for making or publishing of any libel to which a plea of not guilty is entered, the jury may give a general verdict of guilty or not guilty upon the whole trial of indictment matter put in issue on the indictment, and the jury shall not be required or directed by the court to find the person charged guilty merely on the proof of the publication by him of the paper charged to be a libel and of the sense ascribed to such paper in the indictment.

Commencement of jury to give general verdict on trial of indictment for libel.

(2) On every such trial the court shall, according to its discretion, give its opinion and directions to the jury on the matter in issue in like manner as in other criminal cases.

(3) Subsections (1) and (2) of this section shall not operate to prevent the jury from finding a special verdict, in their discretion, as in other criminal cases.

6. On the trial of any indictment for a defamatory libel, the person charged having pleaded such plea as hereinafter mentioned, the truth of the matters charged may be inquired into but shall not amount to a defence, unless it was for the public benefit that the said matters charged should be punished; and, to entitle the defendant to give evidence of the truth of such matters charged as a defence to such indictment, it shall be necessary for the person charged, in pleading to the said indictment, to allege the truth of the said matters charged, in the manner required in pleading a justification to an action for defamation, and further to allege that it was for the public benefit that the said matters charged should be published, and the particular fact or facts by reason of which it was for the public benefit that the said matters charged should be published, to which plea the prosecutor shall be at liberty to reply generally, denying the whole thereof; and if,

Plea of truth of matters charged on trial for defamatory libel and that publication was for public benefit.

after such plea, the person charged is convicted on such indictment, the court may, in pronouncing sentence, consider whether his guilt is aggravated or mitigated by the said plea and by the evidence given to prove or to disprove the same: provided that—

(a) the truth of the matters charged in the alleged libel complained of by such indictment shall in no case be inquired into without such plea of justification;

(b) in addition to such plea of justification, the person charged may enter a plea of not guilty;

(c) nothing in this section shall take away or prejudice any defence under the plea of not guilty which it is competent to the person charged to make under such plea to any indictment for defamatory libel.

Evidence by person charged to rebut prima facie case of publication by his agent.

7. Whenever, upon the trial of an indictment for the publication of a libel, a plea of not guilty having been entered, evidence is given establishing a presumption of publication against the person charged by the act of any other person by his authority, it shall be competent for the person charged to prove that the publication was made without his authority, consent or knowledge and that the publication did not arise from want of due care or caution on his part.

Order of Judge required for prosecution of newspaper proprietor, etc.

8. No criminal prosecution shall be commenced against any proprietor, publisher, editor or any person responsible for the publication of a newspaper for any libel published therein without the order of a Judge of the High Court sitting in camera being first had and obtained, and every application for such order shall be made on notice to the person accused, who shall have an opportunity of being heard against the application.

Inquiry as to libel being for public benefit or being true.

9. A Justice of the District Court, upon the hearing of a charge against a proprietor, publisher or editor or any person responsible for the publication of a newspaper for a libel published therein, may receive evidence as to the publication being for the public benefit, as to the matters charged in the libel being true, as to the report being fair and accurate and published without malice and as to any matter which, under this or any other Act or otherwise, might be given in evidence by way of defence by the person charged on his trial on indictment, and the Justice, if of opinion after hearing such evidence that there is a strong or probable presumption that the jury on the trial would acquit the person charged, may dismiss the case.

10. If a Justice of the District Court, upon the hearing of a charge against a proprietor, publisher, editor or any person responsible for the publication of a newspaper for a libel published therein, is of opinion that, though the person charged is shown to have been guilty, the libel was of a trivial character and that the offence may be adequately punished by virtue of the powers conferred by this section, the Justice shall cause the charge to be reduced into writing and read to the person charged and shall then ask him if he desires to be tried by a jury or consents to the case being dealt with summarily, and, if such person consents to the case being dealt with summarily, may summarily convict him, and impose on him a fine not exceeding fifty pounds, and the Summary Jurisdiction Acts shall apply accordingly.

Provisions as to summary conviction for libel.

11. Every person who maliciously publishes any defamatory libel shall, on conviction thereof on indictment, be liable to a fine not exceeding two hundred pounds or to imprisonment for a term not exceeding one year or to both such fine and imprisonment.

Penalty for maliciously publishing defamatory libel.

12. Every person who maliciously publishes any defamatory libel, knowing the same to be false, shall, on conviction thereof on indictment, be liable to a fine not exceeding five hundred pounds or to imprisonment for a term not exceeding two years or to both such fine and imprisonment.

Penalty for maliciously publishing libel known to be false.

13. (1) Every person who composes, prints or publishes any blasphemous or obscene libel shall, on conviction thereof on indictment, be liable to a fine not exceeding five hundred pounds or to imprisonment for a term not exceeding two years or to both such fine and imprisonment or to penal servitude for a term not exceeding seven years.

Penalty for printing or publishing blasphemous or obscene libel.

(2) (a) In every case in which a person is convicted of composing, printing or publishing a blasphemous libel, the court

may make an order for the seizure and carrying away and detaining in safe custody, in such manner as shall be directed in the order, of all copies of the libel in the possession of such person or of any other person named in the order for his use, evidence upon oath having been previously given to the satisfaction of the court that copies of the said libel are in the possession of such other person for the use of the person convicted.

(b) Upon the making of an order under paragraph (a) of this subsection, any member of the Garda Síochána acting under such order may enter, if necessary by the use of force, and search for any copies of the said libel any building, house or other place belonging to the person convicted or to such other person named in the order and may seize and carry away and detain in the manner directed in such order all copies of the libel found therein.

(c) If, in any such case, the conviction is quashed on appeal, any copies of the libel seized under an order under paragraph (a) of this subsection shall be returned free of charge to the person or persons from whom they were seized.

(d) Where, in any such case, an appeal is not lodged or the conviction is confirmed on appeal, any copies of the libel seized under an order under paragraph (a) of this subsection shall, on the application of a member of the Garda Síochána to the court which made such order, be disposed of in such manner as such court may direct.

PART III

CIVIL PROCEEDINGS FOR DEFAMATION

Interpretation   **14.** (1) In this Part
(Part III)

"broadcast" has the same meaning as in the Wireless Telegraphy Act, 1026 (in this section referred to as the Act of 1926) "broadcasting" shall be construed accordingly;

"broadcasting station" has the same meaning as in the Act of 1926, as amended by the Broadcasting Authority Act, 1960;

"wireless telegraphy" has the same meaning as in the Act of 1926.

(2) Any reference in this Part to words shall be construed as including a reference to visual images, gestures and other methods of signifying meaning.

(3) Where words broadcast by means of wireless telegraphy are simultaneously transmitted by telegraph as defined by the Telegraph Act, 1803, in accordance with a licence granted by the Minister for Posts and Telegraphs, the provisions of this Part shall apply as if the transmission were broadcasting by means of wireless telegraphy.

15. For the purposes of the law of libel and slander the broadcasting of words by means of wireless telegraphy shall be treated as publication in permanent form.

Broadcast statements.

16. Words spoken and published which impute unchastity or adultery to any woman or girl shall not require special damage to render them actionable.

Words imputing unchastity or adultery actionable without special damage.

17. In any action for defamation, it shall be lawful for the defendant (after notice in writing of his intention so to do, duly given to the plaintiff at the time of filing or delivering the plea in evidence in the action) to give in evidence, in mitigation of damage, that he made or offered an apology to the plaintiff for such defamation before the commencement of the action, or as soon afterwards as he had an opportunity of doing so, in case the action shall have been commenced before there was an opportunity of making or offering such apology.

Offer of an apology admissible in evidence in mitigation of damages in action for defamation.

18. (1) A fair and accurate report published in any newspaper or broadcast by means of wireless telegraphy as part of any programme or service provided by means of a broadcasting station within the State or in Northern Ireland of proceedings publicly heard before any court established by law and exercising judicial authority within the State or Northern Ireland shall, if published or broadcast contemporaneously with such proceedings, be privileged.

Newspaper and broadcast report of proceedings in court privileged.

(2) Nothing in subsection (1) of this section shall authorise the publication or broadcasting of any blasphemous or obscene matter.

Slander affecting official, professional or business reputation.

19. In an action for slander in respect of words calculated to disparage the plaintiff in any office, profession, calling, trade or business held or carried on by him at the time of the publication, it shall not be necessary to allege or prove special damage, whether or not the words are spoken of the plaintiff in the way of his office, profession, calling, trade or business.

Slander of title, etc.

20. (1) In an action for slander of title, slander of goods or other malicious falsehood, it shall not be necessary to allege or prove special damage—

(a) if the words upon which the action is founded are calculated to cause pecuniary damage to the plaintiff and are published in writing or other permanent form; or

(b) if the said words are calculated to cause pecuniary damage to the plaintiff in respect of any office, profession, calling, trade or business held or carried on by him at the time of the publication.

(2) Section 15 of this Act shall apply for the purposes of subsection (1) of this section as it applies for the purpose of the law of libel and slander.

Unintentional defamation

21. (1) A person who has published words alleged to be defamatory of another person may, if he claims that the words were published by him innocently in relation to that other person, make an offer of amends under this section, and in any such case—

(a) if the offer is accepted by the party aggrieved and is duly performed, no proceedings for libel or slander shall be taken or continued by that party against the person making the offer in respect of the publication in question (but without prejudice to any cause of action against any other person jointly responsible for that publication);

(b) if the offer is not accepted by the party aggrieved, then, except as otherwise provided by this section, it shall be a defence, in any proceedings by him for libel or slander against the person making the offer in respect of the publication in question, to prove that the words complained of were published by the defendant innocently in relation to the plaintiff and that the offer was made as soon as practicable after the defendant received notice that they were or might be defamatory of the plaintiff, and has not been withdrawn.

(2) An offer of amends under this section must be expressed to be made for the purposes of this section, and must be accompanied by an affidavit specifying the facts relied upon by the person making it to show that the words in question were published by him innocently in relation to the party aggrieved; and for the purposes of a defence under paragraph (h) of subsection (1) of this section no evidence, other than evidence of facts specified in the affidavit, shall be admissible on behalf of that person to prove that the words were so published.

(3) An offer of amends under this section shall be understood to mean an offer—

(a) in any case, to publish or join in the publication of a suitable correction of the words complained of, and a sufficient apology to the party aggrieved in respect of those words;
(b) where copies of a document or record containing the said words have been distributed by or with the knowledge of the person making the offer, to take such steps as are reasonably practicable on his part for notifying persons to whom copies have been so distributed that the words are alleged to be defamatory of the party aggrieved.

(4) Where an offer of amends under this section is accepted by the party aggrieved—

(a) any question as to the steps to be taken in fulfilment of the offer as so accepted shall, in default of agreement between the parties, be referred to and determined by the High Court or, if proceedings in respect of the publication in question have been taken in the Circuit Court, by the Circuit Court, and the decision of such Court thereon shall be final;

(b) the power of the court to make orders as to costs in proceedings by the party aggrieved against the person making the offer in respect of the publication in question, or in proceedings in respect of the offer under paragraph (a) of this subsection, shall include power to order the payment by the person making the offer to the party aggrieved of costs on an indemnity basis and any expenses reasonably incurred or to be incurred by that party in consequence of the publication in question;

and if no such proceedings as aforesaid are taken, the High Court may, upon application made by the party aggrieved, make any such order for the payment of such costs and expenses as aforesaid as could be made in such proceedings.

(5) For the purposes of this section words shall be treated as published by one person (in this subsection referred to as the publisher) innocently in relation to another person if, and only if, the following conditions are satisfied, that is to say—

(a) that the publisher did not intend to publish them of and concerning that other person, and did not know of circumstances by virtue of which they might be understood to refer to him; or
(b) that the words were not defamatory on the face of them and the publisher did not know of circumstances by virtue of which they might be understood to be defamatory of that other person,

and in either case that the publisher exercised all reasonable care in relation to the publication; and any reference in this subsection to the publisher shall be construed as including a reference to any servant or agent of the publisher who was concerned with the contents of the publication.

(6) Paragraph (b) of subsection (1) of this section shall not apply where the party aggrieved proves that he has suffered special damage.

(7) Paragraph (b) of subsection (1) of this section shall not apply in relation to the publication by any person of words of which he is not the author unless he proves that the words were written by the author without malice.

22. In an action for libel or slander in respect of words containing two or more distinct charges against the plaintiff, a defence of justification shall not fail by reason only that the truth of every charge is not proved, if the words not proved to be true do not materially injure the plaintiff's reputation having regard to the truth of the remaining charges.

Justification.

23. In an action for libel or slander in respect of words consisting partly of allegations of fact and partly of expression of opinion, a defence of fair comment shall not fail by reason only that the truth of every allegation of fact is not proved, if the expression of opinion is fair comment having regard to such of the facts alleged or referred to in the words complained of as are proved.

Fair comment.

24. (1) Subject to the provisions of this section, the publication in a newspaper or the broadcasting by means of wireless telegraphy as part of any programme or service provided by means of a broadcasting station within the State or in Northern Ireland of any such report or other matter as is mentioned in the Second Schedule to this Act shall be privileged unless the publication or broadcasting is proved to be made with malice.

Qualified privilege of certain newspaper and broadcasting reports.

(2) In an action for libel in respect of the publication or broadcasting of any such report or matter as is mentioned in Part II of the Second Schedule to this Act, the provisions of this section shall not be a defence if it is proved that the defendant has been requested by the plaintiff to publish in the newspaper in which the original publication was made or to broadcast from the broadcasting station from which the original broadcast was made, whichever is the case, a reasonable statement by way of explanation or contradiction, and has refused or neglected to do so, or has done so in a manner not adequate or not reasonable having regard to all the circumstances.

(3) Nothing in this section shall be construed as protecting the publication or broadcasting of any matter the publication or broadcasting of which is prohibited by law or of any matter which is not of public concern and the publication or broadcasting of which is not for the public benefit

(4) Nothing in this section shall be construed as limiting or abridging any privilege subsisting (otherwise than by virtue of section 4 of the Law of Libel Amendment Act, 1888) immediately before the commencement of this Act.

Agreements for indemnity.

25. An agreement for indemnifying any person against civil liability for libel in respect of the publication of any matter shall not be unlawful unless at the time of the publication that person knows that the matter is defamatory, and does not reasonably believe there is a good defence to any action brought upon it.

Evidence of other damages recovered by plaintiff.

26. In any action for libel or slander the defendant may give evidence in mitigation of damages that the plaintiff has recovered damages, or has brought actions for damages, for libel or slander in respect of the publication of words to the same effect as the words on which the action is founded, or has received or agreed to receive compensation in respect of any such publication.

Obligation on certain newspaper proprietors to be registered under the Registration of Business Names Act, 1916.

27. (1) The proprietor of every newspaper having a place of business in the State shall, where such proprietor is not a company registered under the Companies Acts, 1908 to 1959, and is not required under the provisions of the Registration of Business Names Act, 1916, to be registered under that Act in respect of the business of carrying on such newspaper, be registered in the manner directed by that Act, and that Act shall apply to such proprietor in like manner as it applies to a firm or individual referred to in section 1 thereof.

(2) Every reference in the Registration of Business Names Act, 1916, to that Act shall be construed as a reference to that Act as extended by subsection (1) of this section.

(3) In this section "newspaper" means any paper containing public news or observations thereon, or consisting wholly or

mainly of advertisements, which is printed for sale and is published in the State either periodically or in parts or numbers at intervals not exceeding twenty-six days.

28. Nothing in this Part shall affect the law relating to criminal libel. Saving.

FIRST SCHEDULE Section 4
ENACTMENTS REPEALED
PART I

Acts of the Parliament of Ireland

Session and Chapter	Title
28 Hen. 8, c. 7 (Ir.).	An Act of Slaunder.
2 Geo. 1, c. 20 (Ir.).	An Act to limit the time for Criminal Prosecutions for words spoken.
33 Geo. 3, c. 43 (Ir.).	An Act to remove doubts respecting the functions of juries in cases of libel.

PART II

Acts of the Parliament of the late United Kingdom of Great Britain and Ireland

Session and Chapter	Title
60 Geo. 3 & 1 Geo. 4, c. 8.	Criminal Libel Act, 1819.
3 & 4 Vic., c. 9.	Parliamentary Papers Act, 1840.
6 & 7 Vic., c. 96.	Libel Act, 1843.
8 & 9 Vic., c. 75.	Libel Act, 1845.
32 & 33 Vic., c. 24.	Newspapers Printers and Reading Rooms Repeal Act, 1869.
44 & 45 Vic., c. 60.	Newspaper Libel and Registration Act, 1881.
51 & 52 Vic., c. 64.	Law of Libel Amendment Act, 1888.
54 & 55 Vic., c. 61.	Slander of Women Act, 1891.

SECOND SCHEDULE

STATEMENTS HAVING QUALIFIED PRIVILEGE
PART I

Statements privileged without Explanation or Contradiction

1. A fair and accurate report of any proceedings in public of a
house of any legislature (including subordinate or federal legislatures) of any foreign sovereign State or any body which is part of
such legislature or any body duly appointed by or under the
legislature or executive of such State to hold a public inquiry on a
matter of public importance.

2. A fair and accurate report of any proceedings in public of an
international organization of which the State or the Government is a
member or of any international conference to which the Government sends a representative.

3. A fair and accurate report of any proceedings in public of the
International Court of Justice and any other judicial or arbitral
tribunal deciding matters in dispute between States.

4. A fair and accurate report of any proceedings before a court
(including a courtmartial) exercising jurisdiction under the law of
any legislature (including subordinate or federal legislatures) of
any foreign sovereign State.

5. A fair and accurate copy of or extract from any register kept in
pursuance of any law which is open to inspection by the public or
of any other document which is required by law to be open to
inspection by the public.

6. Any notice or advertisement published by or on the authority
of any court in the State or in Northern Ireland or any Judge or
officer of such a court.

PART II

Statements privileged subject to Explanation or Contradiction

1. A fair and accurate report of the findings or decision of any of the following associations, whether formed in the State or Northern Ireland, or of any committee or governing body thereof, that is to say:

(a) an association for the purpose of promoting or encouraging the exercise of or interest in any art, science, religion or learning, and empowered by its constitution to exercise control over or adjudicate upon matters of interest or concern to the association or the actions or conduct of any persons subject to such control or adjudication;

(b) an association for the purpose of promoting or safeguarding the interests of any trade, business, industry or profession or of the persons carrying on or engaged in any trade, business, industry or profession and empowered by its constitution to exercise control over or adjudicate upon matters connected with the trade, business, industry or profession or the actions or conduct of those persons;

(c) an association for the purpose of promoting or safeguarding the interests of any game, sport or pastime, to the playing or exercise of which members of the public are invited or admitted, and empowered by its constitution to exercise control over or adjudicate upon persons connected with or taking part in the game, sport or pastime;

being a finding or decision relating to a person who is a member of or is subject by virtue of any contract to the control of the association.

2. A fair and accurate report of the proceedings at any public meeting held in the State or Northern Ireland, being a meeting *bona fide* and lawfully held for a lawful purpose and for the furtherance or discussion of any matter of public concern whether the admission to the meeting is general or restricted.

3. A fair and accurate report of the proceedings at any meeting or sitting of—

(a) any local authority, or committee of a local authority or local authorities, and any corresponding authority, or committee thereof, in Northern Ireland;

(b) any Judge or Justice acting otherwise than as a court exercising judicial authority and any corresponding person so acting in Northern Ireland;

(c) any commission, tribunal, committee or person appointed, whether in the State or Northern Ireland, for the purposes of any inquiry under statutory authority;

(d) any person appointed by a local authority to hold a local inquiry in pursuance of an Act of the Oireachtas and any person appointed by a corresponding authority in Northern Ireland to hold a local inquiry in pursuance of statutory authority;

(e) any other tribunal, board, committee or body constituted by or under, and exercising functions under, statutory authority, whether in the State or Northern Ireland;

not being a meeting or sitting admission to which is not allowed to representatives of the press and other members of the public.

4. A fair and accurate report of the proceedings at a general meeting, whether in the State or Northern Ireland, of any company or association constituted, registered or certified by or under statutory authority or incorporated by charter, not being, in the case of a company in Northern Ireland, a private company within tho meaning of the Companies Acts, 1908 to 1959, or, in the case of a company in the State, a private company within the meaning of the statutes relating to companies for the time being in force therein.

5. A copy or fair and accurate report or summary of any notice or other matter issued for the information of the public by or on behalf of any Government department, local authority or the Commissioner of the Garda Síochána or by or on behalf of a corresponding department, authority or officer in Northern Ireland.

A guide to legal terms

for the assistance of journalists

accessory before the fact A person who assists in the commission of a crime by advice or cooperation before the crime is committed.

accessory after the fact A person who, knowing that a crime has been committed, assists the criminal to escape from justice.

accord and satisfaction An established defence in actions, e.g. libel and slander, the essence of which is that the plaintiff has previously agreed to withdraw his action on certain conditions and that the defendant, upon such an undertaking, has fulfilled these conditions.

actus reus The guilty act in a crime.

affidavit A sworn statement in writing.

aggravated damages An increased measure of damages given by a judge or jury where the conduct of the defendant has been so wanton and reckless as to injure the plaintiff to an exceptional degree.

appeal An application to a higher court to revise a decision of an inferior court or tribunal.

Appeal, Court of Criminal A court composed of three superior court judges – one from the Supreme Court and two from the High Court which sits in the Four Courts, Dublin and hears appeals from the Circuit Criminal Court, the Special Criminal Court and the Central Criminal Court. It is also empowered by legislation to refer points of law of 'exceptional public importance' to the Supreme Court for determination.

appellant A person or other entity such as a corporate body at whose instance an appeal is taken.

arson The malicious setting fire to a dwelling house or certain other lands of property.

Attorney General The chief legal adviser to the Government

attorney, power of A written authority given by one person to another to act legally in his name.

bail Money deposited or pledged to ensure a person's appearance before a court.

bailee A person with whom property is pledged or deposited, e.g. a pawnbroker.

blasphemy The offence of reviling or ridiculing the accepted tenets of religion. An element of criminal libel.

brief The written instructions prepared by solicitors for barristers conducting cases before courts or tribunals.

certiorari A writ ordering the removal of a trial from one court to another, e.g. from an inferior to a higher court. If the applicant is successful, the court may quash the order made by the inferior tribunal.

case stated A statement of facts prepared by a court in order to get the opinion of a higher court on a point of law.

Central Criminal Court The High Court exercising its criminal jurisdiction.

contempt of court Conduct offensive to a court or prejudicial to the administration of justice.

copyright The exclusive right to make copies of an original work.

counsel Barristers, including Senior Counsel, and members of the Junior Bar.

criminal libel A libel so grave or so dangerous a character, that it is the fit subject of criminal proceedings.

damages, general Such damages as the law presumes to have resulted from a civil wrong (a tort) without the plaintiff having to prove special injury.

damages, special Direct loss and damage as the plaintiff can prove he suffered as a result of the defendant's wrongful conduct.

defamation The publication of words injurious to another person's character or reputation.

discovery A legal proceeding in the Circuit Court or High Court by which a party to a civil action is ordered to disclose on oath any documents in his possession or procurement bearing on the issue in dispute.

exemplary damages The awarding of damages that are so heavy as to make an example of a defendant.

ex-parte **proceedings** Proceedings conducted on behalf of one party to a civil action in the absence of the other.

fair comment Just and reasonable comment on matters of public interest.

felony A term applied to some serious forms of crime which attract a prison sentence.

habeas corpus An order by the High Court directing a person such as a prison authority or a Garda Síochána to bring a prisoner before the court to justify the grounds of his or her detention.

injunction An order of a civil court (excluding the District Court) commanding the performance of or the prohibition of some act, disobedience to which is punishable as contempt of court.

innuendo The interpretation placed by the plaintiff on words which are the subject of an action for damages for libel.

intra vires Within the power of.

justification A defence to an action for damages for libel which obliges the plaintiff to prove the truth of the libel.

libel A permanent representation such as writing the effect of which is to injure a person's good name by holding him up to public ridicule, hatred or contempt.

mandamus A writ issued by a higher to a lower court ordering it to perform some duty.

misdemeanour A less serious form of crime which does not amount to a felony.

notary public An officer of the court, usually a solicitor in practice, authorized to certify deeds, contracts, affidavits and other legal documents.

onus of proof The burden of proof is the obligation to prove a set of facts by evidence. In a civil action, the plaintiff must prove his case on the balance of probabilities; in a criminal prosecution, the prosecution must prove the accused's guilt beyond a reasonable doubt.

plaintiff The party who brings the complaint in a civil action.

pleadings The documents exchanged between the parties to a civil action during the preparation of the case for trial.

prima facie On a first view; a *prima facie* case is one which raises a presumption of the accused's guilt sufficient that he or she be sent forward for trial.

privilege A special legal right or immunity.

punitive damages Damages which are so great or so heavy as to punish a defendant in a civil action whose conduct has been of a flagrant nature and a gross infringement of the plaintiff's right.

recognizances An undertaking given to a court to do or not to do a particular act, e.g. to appear at a future date, or to be of good behaviour for a stated period. Breach of the undertaking can lead to forfeiture of a certain sum.

sine die A Latin phrase meaning 'without a day'. It is used when legal proceedings are adjourned indefinitely. The term is normally associated with inquests at the Coroner's Court.

slander Defamatory words uttered by word of mouth.

solicitor A lawyer who conducts general legal business, manages law suits and instructs counsel in court.

specific performance A legal remedy granted against a defendant which directs him to perform a contract in the plaintiff's favour.

sub judice The term applied when legal proceedings have been commenced, any public comment on which is contempt of court.

subpoena A summons addressed to a witness ordering his attendance in court for the hearing of an action.

surety A person who goes bail for another.

ultra vires A Latin phrase meaning outside or beyond the power, applied e.g. when a local authority exceeds its legal powers or a court or tribunal its jurisdiction.

without prejudice The phrase used in relation to a letter written or an admission made in the course of negotiations, on the understanding that will not be used against the party making it in the event of an action at law.

Index